INCENTIVE TRAVEL

FOR A NEW WORLD

PATRICK PATRIDGE

Dr. Patrick Patridge

ISBN 9798459291858

Cover design: Art Painter
Frontispiece: © Paula Patridge-Neumann
Photos: © Dr. Patrick Patridge
Library of Congress Control Number: 2018675309
Published in the United States of America

DEDICATION

This book is kindly dedicated to my MICE Muses
Heike Mahmoud, Barbara Jamison, Alexandra Nitze
Marina Parra-Flechsig
Annamaria Ruffini and Daisy Zhang

And to my Incentive Travel Mentors
Werner Dresel, Patrick Delaney, J.J. Gubbins
and Hugo Slimbrouck

In Memoriam
Miek Egberts

PREFACE

There will always be changes in our world and the way that we do business, the way that we travel, the way that we experience destinations and the way that we celebrate success.

What will remain a constant, though, is the human desire to celebrate that success, and to incentivize each other through extraordinary experiences.

Working in the Incentive Travel industry is truly one of the most motivating and rewarding industries that I could imagine working in.

Like so many of us, I am always looking for new educational content to keep myself abreast of best practices in our marketplace and I am so thrilled to see a book of this nature being launched.

Dr. Patrick Patridge has been an active SITE member for over 30 years. This is a huge commitment to our Association, and we are so grateful for his support.

I am so proud to see a fellow SITE member become a published author.

Aoife Delaney

President

SITE - Society for Incentive Travel Excellence

CONTENTS

LIST OF ABBREVIATIONS

AV - Audio-Visual

CITP - Certified Incentive Travel Professional

CIS - Certified Incentive Travel Specialist

CSR - Corporate Social Responsibility

CVB - Convention and Visitor Bureau

DMC - Destination Management Company

DMO - Destination Marketing Organisation

MICE - Meetings, Incentives, Conferences, Events

RFP - Request for Proposal

SITE - Society for Incentive Travel Excellence

USP - Unique Selling Proposition

UVP - Unique Value Proposition

INTRODUCTION

"Great journeys are never about the destination."

Benjamin Myers in *'The Offing'*.

The *Society for Incentive Travel Excellence* (SITE) was founded on the 4th of December 1973 in the *'Americana'* hotel in New York City.

Since then, Incentive Travel has slowly but surely spread all around the globe - reflected today by SITE membership in some ninety countries worldwide.

SITE defines Incentive Travel as:

"A global management tool that uses an exceptional travel experience to motivate and / or recognize participants for increased levels of performance in sup-

port of organisational goals."

Its tagline being:

Incentive Travel. Business Results.

Incentive Travel in the company of colleagues or customers is a special, complex, and emotional journey.

The Incentive Travel story is an inspired narrative that is curated for the mind, but felt with the heart.

It is not something which can be purchased ready-to-wear.

It is either *couture* or tailor-made.

Companies and organisations who wish to produce, direct and stage customised Incentive Travel programmes (i.e., *unique travel experiences which cannot be bought from a tour operator online or over a travel agent's counter*) require expert local advice and experienced partners with best-practice ideas and collaborative networking, communications and trip delivery skills.

The Covid crisis and its *caesura* have had traumatic impacts on the worlds of work and travel.

It is imperative, therefore, for all engaged in the Incentive Travel industry to carefully consider how we can recuperate, re-connect, re-boot and thrive by becoming active, relevant and prosperous once again.

Finding a restorative medium between gravitational pull and centrifugal force, so to say.

This book is not an academic treatise.

The aim of this book is to offer subjects and themes that may provide readers with food for thought and pertinent inspiration for what I have termed:

Incentive Travel for a New World.

So, imagine that you are starting from "GO" in a game of *Monopoly*.

"GO" marks the border between our worlds pre-Covid and post-Covid.

Questions will have to be asked, answers provided, and critical decisions taken.

Such as:

- *What will remain?*

- *What will change?*

- *How will change manifest itself?*

- *How can we re-adapt?*

- *Where should investment occur?*

- *How can we assist one another?*

In many respects, much appears as if the wheel has

come full circle.

Somewhat.

Because my inaugural contact with Incentive Travel was way back in March 1990 at a packed *ITB Berlin* morning talk about *"Individual Incentives"* - given by SITE Past-President, J.J. Gubbins from Chicago, at the time *Vice-President Incentives* at *The Sheraton Corporation.*

Since then, *Individual Incentives* have become the almost exclusive preserve of global gift voucher corporations and online shopping platforms.

Could there be potential right now, however, for *"hybrid / stop-gap"* individual incentive solutions to bridge the post-Covid group travel chasm?

With, for example, 40 qualifiers enjoying Individual Incentive Travel experiences in their home localities and regions, instead of them all coming together in one place or city abroad, as they would have done pre-Covid.

Continuing, however, to fulfil self-financing organisational and corporate goals such as those outlined in the SITE Foundation *"Report on Incentive Travel in Europe"*:

- *Increased individual productivity.*

- *Improved employee and customer engagement.*

- Enhanced customer satisfaction.

- Improved customer & employee retention.

- Better relationship-building between employees & management.

Serving to re-boot our industry with health & safety compliant, small but *"distanced"* Incentive Travel groups.

"Back to Basics", so to say - with apparently ordinary little things taking on new meaning and significance.

Further training and education gaining added *momentum*.

Reviving Incentive Travel by creating purposeful, memorable, and motivating experiences for our unpredictable times.

And moving on from there to define anew moments that may still be pivotal for personal, business, and scientific success.

And not only for *"Traditional Qualifiers"* from branches such as Finance & Insurance, Automotive, Pharmaceuticals and Consumer Electronics.

But also, for *"System-Relevant Beneficiaries"* from sectors such as Health Care, Food & Retail, Community Care, Transport & Logistics, Child-Minding, Teaching, Civil Defence & Emergency Services.

Generating sound emotional experiences that rise above newly engendered post-Covid routines, making trip participants feel recognised, rewarded, happy and healthy once again.

Laying foundations for landmark transitions to post-"*Lockdown*" lifestyles, education and workplace *scenarios*.

Corona Virus - together with *Climate Crisis* - in the words of Irish Nobel Prize-winning poet, William Butler Yeats, means that:

"*All changed, changed utterly*:

A *terrible beauty is born*."

'Easter, 1916'

Incentive Travel professionals have traditionally taken a holistic view of our calling - giving priority to in-tangibles such as connection, engagement, motivation and relationship-building.

This mindset will remain a source of fortitude and strength as we transition to a *New World* but NOT a "*New Normal*".

Because there is no New Normal.

Serving as a stimulus to master current challenges and future crises together by adopting tried-and-trusted and traditional remedies *in tandem* with dynamic and unforeseen post-Covid Incentive Travel solutions.

Our industry has always had to adapt to changing parameters and external circumstances - not all of them positive or beneficial (e.g., *Banking Crises, Economic Recessions, Terrorism, Wars, Natural & Human Catastrophes*).

Incentive Travel should, however, remain an important component of future motivational events because it has been proven to work.

Time and again.

And given half a century's experience to fall back upon - and our industry's indelible enthusiasm and boundless energy - Incentive Travel should be confidently re-deployed in unanticipated and welcome new directions.

This book serves as a small contribution for collegial discussion, industry debate and as an *impetus* for optimistic engagement and affirmative thinking.

It calls for Incentive Travel to be re-defined post-Covid as:

"A very special tool that uses an exceptional travel experience to motivate, recognize and / or reward individuals for exemplary levels of engagement, performance and achievement in support of either organisational, scientific, climate, environmental or societal goals."

Dr. Patrick Patridge

Note to readers:

You can read this book either from start to finish or you can dip in and out of individual chapters and subjects as you please.

Links to Best-Practice, Topical Research and Select Trade Press are listed at the end of the book.

QR Codes throughout lead you directly to web landing-pages and to *YouTube* videos which you can scan and open on your mobile devices.

Exercises at the end of chapters encourage you to contemplate, discuss and co-create.

QUO VADIS?

Corporations in Europe were already re-evaluating the benefits of traditional Incentive Travel for their strategic goals and concerns pre-Covid.

Concrete business results instead of memorable experiences were often the currency of the day.

Corporate Goals included:

- *Reward and recognition for sales performance.*

- *Attracting new employees and retaining staff.*

- *Familiarizing staff with new markets.*

- *Familiarizing distributors with new products.*

- *Getting to know business partners better.*

- Getting to know customers better.

- Promoting brand loyalty and corporate identity.

- Identifying new business opportunities.

- Re-adjusting after mergers and takeovers.

German clients, for instance, were already looking for fiscally compliant events, factory visits, individual travel experiences and vocational training as opposed to classic *"team building"* and *"luxury"* activities.

German MICE agencies were suggesting programmes in destinations with a *"quirky"* ambience and *"idiosyncratic"* atmosphere - such as Bilbao in Spain and Riga in Latvia.

The latter trend partly a result of increasing qualifier travel sophistication, online booking platforms, low-cost flights, high-speed rail, and affordable tour operator packages to popular cities such as Amsterdam, Lisbon and Barcelona.

Incentive-Intense Branches

Incentive Travel remains specific to the plans, needs, and requirements of particular branches. It is important to understand this from the outset.

In fashion industry terms, it is custom-fit and *boutique.*

Challenges in the areas of management, marketing,

sales, distribution, and personnel are still as far-reaching and varied as ever before in the worlds of Finance & Insurance, Automotive, Consumer Electronics and Pharmaceuticals - traditionally the most relevant branches for Incentive Travel activity.

(See APPENDIX I).

Goals common to these incentive-intense branches include:

Increasing turnover, growing business, maintaining relationships, and *inspiring loyalty.*

(See APPENDIX II).

Incentive Travel for these branches will continue to be carefully conceived and expertly planned post-Covid - irrespective of tighter budgets, lower frequency, and shorter duration in the *interim.*

The inclusion of *family members and partners* will become more important - with additional time set aside for beneficiaries / qualifiers to catch-up, chill-out and recuperate with family and loved ones.

Indeed, travel may not always be the solution in this *scenario* - but it is still to be highly recommended all the same.

Individual Travel Incentives, cash *boni,* personal vouchers and gift cards will continue to play a significant role.

See, for example, the success of corporate gift card suppliers such as *amazon incentives.*

Growth Sectors

Buoyant sectors (*Leibnitz Centre for European Economic Research*) with high potential for post-Covid Incentive Travel include:

- *Electronics*

- *Chemicals*

- *Green Energy*

- *Mechanical Engineering*

- *Food Science*

- *Aerospace*

- *Information Technology*

- *Biomedical Technology*

Our immediate task as Incentive Travel specialists is to identify *operative, research, tactical and strategic goals* in these growth sectors and devise offerings that will dovetail with - accompany and complement these.

System-Relevant Beneficiaries / Qualifiers will include persons whose contributions are strategically weighted and considered intrinsically important to the achievement of overall organisational and corporate success.

They will not only include traditional management, sales, dealer & distribution personnel (*Qualifiers*) - but also back-office, cyber-security, research & development, health & safety, product testing, teachers & training staff (*System-Relevant Beneficiaries*).

This exciting *scenario* will, however, require a significant shift from traditional *"Winner Takes it All"* qualifier mindsets, to *"Sense of Achievement"*, system-relevant mindsets.

This is where *business potential* and *bedrock motivation* may subsequently be found - and where a host of compelling and untapped Incentive Travel opportunities may exist.

QR Code: *ZEW - Leibnitz Centre for Economic Research in Mannheim*

ITII - Incentive Travel Industry Index

SITE CMO Pádraic Gilligan reports in his *Padrai-cino.com* post from 23rd April 2021 that Incentive Travel programmes pre-Covid (*ITII 2019*) were, on aggregate, primarily structured around cultural and group dining experiences, team building and luxury.

A programme was designed as a win / win for qualifiers who got a brilliant travel experience - and corporate client sponsor, who got a better-connected workforce.

When compared with the *ITII 2020*, however, a new and more purposeful incentive travel model was seen to be emerging.

Luxury and cultural experiences remained in the Top 4 rankings, but group dining and team building were replaced by CSR and Wellness.

The rise of CSR, according to Gilligan, highlights changing priorities post-Covid as corporations continue to favour travel as part of their reward and recognition programmes, placing emphasis on the intrinsic joy of travel and putting qualifiers centre stage.

"Building programmes around rejuvenation, destination discovery and delight, all peppered by notions of responsible travel and giving back to communities."

Future Incentive Travel

Future Incentive Travel could help sharpen strategic thinking, problem-solving, inter-personal and communications skills.

It could create *time & space* for clients, beneficiaries / qualifiers, and trip participants to:

- *Manage virtual workloads and home-offices.*

- *Get more involved in decision-making processes.*

- *Discover sustainable solutions to future concerns.*

- *Feel comfortable with new technologies.*

- *Blossom in an environment of co-creation.*

- *Achieve life-learning and work-life-balance.*

- *Acquire, practice and perfect necessary new skills.*

- *Resolve research problems and internal conflicts.*

- *Face challenges as highly motivated teams.*

- *Help the best and brightest become even more so.*

- *Provide opportunities to refresh and to reflect.*

- *Enjoy appreciation for performance achieved.*

- *Sow seeds for creativity & innovation.*

Core skills, attitudes and competencies that may be required from future Incentive Travel participants include:

- *Having a curious and open-minded disposition.*

- *Keeping a clear perspective in complex situations.*

- *Being able to handle change and diversity easily.*

- *Possessing an ability to network and to influence.*

* * * * *

"In the future, incentive trips will remain relevant for achieving meaningful goals only if the travel share is clearly-defined and closely-tailored to client messages and goals and when results can be effectively monitored and controlled."

Kinga Wagner

China and India

Of particular interest post-Covid are developments in the rapidly growing and globally expanding Chinese and Indian markets for outbound Incentive Travel.

Recent research from *VisitBritain* has, for instance, highlighted what Chinese planners seek when visiting Europe:

- *Themed gala dinners / awards nights*

- *Team building activities*

- *Meetings and training sessions*

- *Sightseeing in iconic scenery*

- *Mix of Chinese and destination cuisine*

- *Cultural events / local immersion*

- *Shopping opportunities*

- *Corporate social responsibility*

- *Iconic group photo locations*

The Middle Kingdom or China should be a key driver of economic recovery and of future growth in the 21st century.

So, keep a close eye on key developments there, and in India, too - and do your best to listen to, understand and learn all about what is deemed relevant and important to Chinese and Indian clients, planners, and trip participants.

Climate Protection and Incentive Travel

2020 was one of the three warmest years on record. Our planet has heated up by 1.2 degrees *Celsius* since industrialisation (*State of the Global Climate Report of the World Weather Organization 2021*).

Temperatures in Europe reached a record, with 48.8 degrees *Celsius* recorded on Thursday, 12th August 2021 in Sicily.

CO_2 in the atmosphere, sea levels and ocean temperatures have also reached new record values. Arctic Sea ice has shrunk to the second smallest area ever measured in summertime.

Researchers have also discovered that the North Atlantic Gulf Stream current system is weaker than at any time over the past 1,000 years. Its collapse would substantially cool Europe and have drastic consequences for the Incentive Travel industry.

As I write, forest fires are raging in Algeria, California, Greece, Southern Italy, Russia and Turkey. Floods have devastated communities in Austria, Benelux, China, Germany, Turkey, Japan, and Korea.

So, as SITE enters its sixth decade, we will witness increasing engagement in the fields of biodiversity, environment and climate protection.

Solutions to these problems will be sought globally in a variety of live, hybrid and virtual communication platforms and events involving future-oriented and highly networked individuals.

Financial TV journalist, Sina Mainitz, reported in *heute JOURNAL Börse Nachrichten* (German stock exchange news, 13th August 2021) that climate-friendly products are still very much a niche.

While the volume of investment in Germany in climate-friendly products grew by one third in the years 2019 - 2021, they still account for only 6.4% of the total German stock market volume, i.e., 248 billion Euros of 3,850 billion Euros.

In the long run, according to Mainitz, *Green Investments* will, however, prevail, and investors will invest in climate-friendly products. Experts forecast that only such companies will be sustainable and able to secure future jobs.

Our industry should position itself to assist in any way possible and play its part to the full.

QR Code: *State of the Global Climate 2020*

SITE Global Conference 2022 in Dublin

Ample opportunities will be presented to discuss all of the above - and much more indeed - at the *SITE Global Conference 2022* in my home city of Dublin - on the occasion of the 25th Anniversary of the establishment of *SITE Ireland*.

QR Code: *SITE Global Conference 2022*

* * * * *

So, it's high time for us all to get back to our drawing boards, come up with - and co-create - imaginative and pertinent programmes that will not only meet - but exceed the needs and requirements of 21st century Incentive Travel.

As my U.C.D. Geography Professor, Tom Jones Hughes, used to say at the conclusion of all his lectures:

"Life is short. This is it!"

So, there is no time like the present.

Exercise:

1. How can Incentive Travel planners assist host destinations in their Climate Protection efforts?

2. Discuss, budget, and design an Incentive Travel programme for "System-Relevant Beneficiaries" (e.g., from health care, emergency services, medical research, teaching staff) - bearing in mind that these trips might not be "self-financing" as are trips for traditional Qualifiers (e.g., from automotive, insurance, consumer electronics, pharmaceuticals).

3. What funding is available to pay for or subsidize system-relevant Incentive Travel programmes? (e.g., corporate, state, federal, communal, CSR, charity, crowdfunding).

THE BUSINESS CASE

"How would you feel if you had the best Business Case in town for Corporate Incentive Travel?"

Traditionally, three key factors were needed for an Incentive Travel programme to be successful:

- *Easy accessibility.*

- *Quality hotel accommodation* (including food & beverages).

- *Excellent value for money.*

Memorable moments were the *"creative touches"* and *"aha"* experiences that surprised and delighted qualifiers.

These moments defined an Incentive Travel programme as an authentic and extraordinary travel experience offered in recognition of personal and / or team performance.

A growing number of corporate decision-makers are increasingly seeking Incentive Travel destinations that are aligned to their commercial branch and business activity.

A fundamental question that should always be asked is:

What does the client wish to achieve by running an Incentive Travel programme in the first place?

The Business Case Rationale

A good example of contemporary Business Case thinking is the *CAMP X by Volvo Group* mission statement:

"By establishing CampX by Volvo Group we will drive the transformation to new disruptive business models and technologies, with a focus on automation, electromobility and connectivity."

DMOs, CVBs and DMCs should understand and absorb such overarching business goals before bidding for Incentive Travel business or responding to RFPs.

Sightseeing, shopping, and sporting activities may not actually be desired; rather visits to technical facilities, factory production units and university research departments.

Topped off by informal evening get-togethers in suitably themed locations where researchers, developers, distributors, and sales forces come together to talk shop.

A good example of a *Thematic Context Setting* for the above is the *Lindholmen Science Park* in the smart and sustainable city of Gothenburg.

This is a dynamic arena for international collaboration across borders and home to several of Sweden's leading development projects - with a particular focus on future mobility.

Lessons may be learnt there about the creation and diffusion of ideas, new technologies and global trends - fields of Swedish expertise since the pioneering days of *University of Lund* Professors Torsten E. Hägerstrand and Gunnar Törnqvist.

Other examples of thematic context settings include the *VW Autostadt* in Wolfsburg, Germany, the *Microsoft Campus* in Dublin, Ireland, and the *London Fashion Centre*, in London, UK.

Bearing the Swedish example in mind, Incentive Travel experts should develop *Incentive Travel Business Cases* that explain in detail why companies and organisations from any given branch should organise Incentive Travel to their destinations.

This will support differentiation (*both domestic and international*), enabling destinations to distinguish themselves from their competitors and facilitate clearer decision-making on the part of clients.

Business Cases should be subsequently tweaked for specific client objectives and carefully incorporated into and / or reflected in Incentive Travel programmes on the ground, when and wherever appropriate.

Everything you do must link back to the prevailing goals in key customer branches and organisations, otherwise the Incentive Travel experience could be superfluous for the clients and meaningless to trip participants.

Your *Incentive Travel Business Cases* are USPs and UVPs that you should feature prominently in RFP submissions, sales pitches and trade exhibition presentations at

e.g., *AIME, Conventa, IMEX Frankfurt, IBTM World, IMEX America, ITB Berlin, International Confex, ITB China, ITE & MICE.*

They should appear selectively on customised web landing pages, social media posts, news releases and appointment requests.

So, shout them from the rooftops!

Stakeholders and relevant staff should also be briefed - ensuring that all actors are finely tuned with core concerns and key messages.

Your clients and their Incentive Travel beneficiaries / qualifiers will be eminently inspired - and, indeed, most suitably impressed!

QR Code: *Camp X* **by Volvo Group**

QR Code: *Lindholmen Science Park*

Exercise:

1. Research corporate Mission Statements that reveal goals and objectives that could assist you in creating compelling Business Cases for Incentive Travel.

2. Compile a list of Thematic Context Settings suitable for specific clients and branches.

CORE TRENDS

"How would you like to be considered a dedicated follower of fashion?"

Brian Solis in his bestselling book, "*The End of Business as Usual: Rewire the way you work to succeed in the consumer revolution*", states that:

"We should explore acts of increasing customer engagement as a way of cultivating meaningful and productive experiences. It is through the generation of positive experiences that we can assure the materialization of other important business drivers such as sales, referrals, acquisition, and retention costs. More importantly, we can ensure relevance."

This is a wonderful maxim for what Incentive Travel is

all about.

What follows is a *synopsis* of Core Trends in Germany pre-Covid.

Trends that retain much of their inherent validity today.

At the outset, however, destinations, suppliers and DMCs should reflect that what they often considered exceptional programme delivery was sometimes not considered to be exceptional at all.

Exceptional trip delivery was what defined travel programmes for qualifiers as extraordinary experiences offered because of their own exceptional work engagement and past performance.

Corporate clients and incentive agencies had come to expect exceptional trip delivery as *par for the course* in all of their dealings with DMOs, CVBs, and DMCs.

Traditional Incentive Travel markets in the U.S.A. and Western Europe were becoming saturated in branches such as automotive and insurance.

An *"uneasy"* sense of entitlement was felt to prevail among many repeat qualifiers.

Such extraordinary performers had long ago learnt to join in all the dots and fill in all the gaps.

It was difficult to continually come up with something exciting and new to top last year's incentive - something to knock participants' socks off and impress their significant others, neighbours, and colleagues once again.

Some qualifiers had, to state it quite frankly, been spoilt by success and far too many exceptional Incentive Travel experiences.

Social, economic and climate challenges post-Covid may, however, be just what the doctor ordered.

Bringing it all back home, so to say - with *"Post-Covid Reality Checks"*.

All the while, contemplating Incentive Travel possibilities and solutions for both traditional branches and for exciting new realms of forward-thinking economic enterprise and scientific research.

Core Trends In Germany Pre-Covid

Or - *"The Baker's Dozen"*

1. *Preferred DMC partners* were mostly used when organising events abroad. Agencies tended to remain quite loyal to established partners over a long period of time.

2. Was, however, *special expertise* required that was not available from an established DMC partner, agencies were quite willing to enter new DMC relationships.

3. Reliable and *speedy air access with MICE terms and conditions* from key international airports was considered essential due to shorter programme duration and increased time constraints (e.g., *Deutsche Lufthansa Meetings & Events*).

4. Friendly and warm hospitality was considered a *sine qua non*.

5. Tips for *"hip"* and *"unusual"* venues, affordable, three- to four-star hotels with a personal touch (*compliance regulations / pharma codex*), and *"in"* pubs and restaurants.

These had to be plentiful to highlight the *"attractiveness"*, *"uniqueness"* and *"saleability"* of an Incentive Travel destination.

6. Planners wished to be kept regularly informed about changes, new investments and future developments.

7. Sunshine was popular (*e.g., Greece, Spain, Italy, and Portugal*) but not necessarily essential (*e.g., Poland, Denmark, Ireland and Scotland*).

8. Suggestions for *outdoor programme possibilities* in the rural and natural environs of larger cities - with tips for extramural excursions, seminar locations and half-day sporting / team activities.

9. When promoting events, it was important for destinations to deliver fully thought-through concepts with transparent and detailed cost breakdowns - the

latter considered vital for corporate financial con-trollers, compliance, and procurement departments.

10. Indeed, such *"non-MICE"* decision-makers formed an increasingly important part of Incentive Travel deci-sion-making processes – as did *Sustainability* and *CSR Officers* (particularly in *stock exchange-noted* compan-ies).

11. In view of tighter and / or shrinking budgets in many branches, the primary challenge for destinations and suppliers was to deliver targeted, safe, high-qual-ity, value for money and top-notch proposals with flex-ible options on moderate budgets.

i.e., Incentive Travel that did not only satisfy client re-quirements, but which also generated authentic, mem-orable, and personalised experiences, positive publicity and a demand for future activity - whether these were full-scale dealer incentives or corporate meetings and retreats with an *"Incentive Travel"* touch.

Not always easy to supply at the drop of a hat, espe-cially given the fact that client enquiry lead-in times were getting shorter all the time.

12. Corporate client RFPs were frequently sent to an average of three incentive agencies who then - often for compliance reasons - sent them on to another three DMCs / hotels / venues.

This often meant up to nine DMCs or hotels receiving an original RFP – some receiving the same RFP twice or three times over.

13. Content, creativity, understanding of client objectives and goals, and value for money within a set budget per participant were what - at the end of the day - decided for a particular destination / DMC / hotel.

* * * * *

German Corporate Clients, it should also be noted, often booked accommodation and flights via in-house travel departments, requiring only local programme support, transport, and activity services from a DMC.

Some 75% of German incentive agencies, for example, were primarily involved with domestic business, while up to 25% operated in the international sphere - often with clients whose trade and business was of a global nature.

Corporate meetings, congresses and technical visits were on the rise in pre-Covid Germany, with classic Incentive Travel declining except in the traditional automotive and insurance branches – a situation further complicated by stricter tax, procurement, and compliance parameters and by safety concerns (*terrorist attacks*) when travelling abroad.

An additional problem for many German incentive agencies was that the cake was not growing, but the number of competing agencies was - a situation mirrored in many other countries.

This *"onion-peel effect"* increased competition among agencies whose staff - compared to the previous decade - had often been reduced by up to one-half.

The Covid crisis led not only to a major cessation of business and requests in 2020 / 2021 but also to further agency consolidation, staff shortages and business closures (*in the hospitality sector in particular*).

Enquiries for 2022 and 2023 are, however, looking quite good.

Nonetheless, we will have to wait and see how business on the ground actually transpires.

Using our collective energy in the meantime to promote continued desire and demand for Incentive Travel and to educate ourselves - so that our industry is ready to *rock 'n roll* as suitable opportunities present themselves once again.

Exercise:

1. What were the Core Incentive Travel Trends pre-Covid in your key branches and source markets?

2. How are you going to continue to service, supply and satisfy clients from key branches and markets post-Covid?

MILLENNIALS AND GENERATION Y

Millennials or Generation Y is the demographic following so-called Generation X (*1964-1980*).

Researchers and commentators use birth years ranging from 1980 to the early 2000s.

Bearing in mind all other information about the Incentive Travel market, and trends both national and global, it is worth taking time to understand what may be relevant to this generation of Incentive Travel actors.

A generation that is said to seek *authenticity over luxury, local over global, diversity over uniformity.*

A generation that is causing global players to radically disrupt and alter their business models, stripping themselves of generic corporate branding and presenting themselves as *"local service providers"* once again.

When they travel, Generation Y wish to stay in hotels where there is a *colourful and vibrant local scene.*

In *"Hip and Happening Places"* such as Antwerpen, Barcelona, Berlin, Copenhagen, Edinburgh, Helsinki, Istanbul, Galway, Ljubljana, Liverpool, Milano, Paris, Porto, Reykjavik, Sevilla, St. Petersburg and Warsaw - or simply just, "*Alternatives Wien*".

Millennials want to be treated and served like local residents *(if at all possible)* and experience destinations from the inside out.

Generation Y travellers seek *absorbing, personal and enlightening experiences of life and of times today.*

They are curious to get inside *a destination's personality.*

At the same time, WLAN *or* Wi-Fi *connectivity* is very important, so they seek locations where they can also sit, surf, work & communicate with their social media and business networks.

Digital nomads on the move.

Destinations and DMCs are challenged to look beyond popular visitor attractions and activities and to incorporate something of their uniqueness and idiosyncrasies into Generation Y Incentive Travel experiences.

Finally, one should bear in mind that Generation Y will not only make up an increasing number of Incentive Travel beneficiaries / qualifiers but will comprise an increasing number of Incentive Travel actors from decision-makers and planners to DMCs and hoteliers.

It is, therefore, necessary that destinations, DMCs and suppliers suitably communicate with and serve Generation Y customers and colleagues when, where and how they wish to be addressed.

Integrated and state-of-the-art online communications, reservations, and feedback platforms - paralleled by a host of social media options readily available over every type of desktop and mobile device will be required.

While at the same time, not forgetting or ignoring the needs and requirements of Generation X and of the soon-to-be retiring, *Baby Boomers* (1955 - 1964).

And while the virtual world will take on a veritable life of its own, the personal approach will, on the other hand, become even more significant.

Good people, enthralling stories, and interpersonal skills will be in demand as much as ever.

And in future, too, we will also have to consider *Generation Z* born after the year 2000, a generation of *"digital natives"* that already accounts for 40% of consumers globally.

A generation that is gaining headline attention with *#FridaysForFuture* and the sharing economy. A generation, who do not owe loyalty to brands, but who have come to expect personalised digital experiences that cut through all the static.

Exercise:

1. How do the Incentive Travel requirements of Baby Boomers, Generation X, Generation Y, and Generation Z differ?

SCRIPT FOR MILLENNIALS

"Wouldn't it be cool to have bench-mark Millennial Scripts that enlighten and inspire?"

What follows is a lyrical *"Script for Millennials"*.

It serves as a handy little template for Millennial Incentive Travel - whether for Boston, Buenos Aires, Beijing, Bangkok, Capetown, Melbourne, Paris, New York, London, San Francisco, Singapore, Tokio or Rome ...

Incentive Travel for Millennials will remain a question of enthusiasm, knowledge, sympathy, authenticity, and approach - irrespective of circumstances and context.

And this mindset will help sustain us as we set out to navigate post-Covid challenges and uncertain times.

NB - *Readers are urged to study* SITE Crystal Award Winners' *programmes. These are a tremendous source of inspiration, best-practice and encouragement.*

QR Code: *SITE Crystal Award Winners*

A Script For Millennials - Munich

Renowned for *Dirndl, Lederhosen, Oktoberfest.*

München - or Munich - possesses a distinct under-standing of Millennial motivation & leisure time needs.

And Munich has a cool story – or several cool stories, to tell.

Of trendy locations, stylish encounters, and meaning-ful experiences.

Like its famous beers, Munich is a city with character and warm personality.

Where you can quietly feel at home and in no time

at all enjoy fantastic team spirit with colleagues and friends – some of them old, many now new.

Learning while doing.

Munich is a city of amazing contrasts.

Grand and profane, traditional, high-tech ...

Ingrained with beauty, consciousness, culture, diversity.

Engaged, entertaining, fashionable, innovative, musical ...

Parks, shops, sports, restaurants, theatres.

Sensations and styles ...

Swift-flowing *Isar, Deutsches Museum.*

Soak up atmosphere and buzz in *Glockenbach, Maxvorstadt, Schlachthof* and *Schwabing.*

Especially in summer, what with street cafés, open-air cinemas, rooftop bars, music festivals and dare we mention it, "*Mediterranean Flair*".

Enjoy the views - and on fine clear days, splendid glimpses of majestic Bavarian Alps.

Activity, discourse, fresh air, excitement & fun - pop-up stores on *Odeonsplatz* - high-wire climbing in *Grün-*

wald - Jochen Schweizer's body-flying, wave-surfing, levitating-foxes in *Taufkirchen!*

And if you visit in August, one happening you should not miss is *Munich Summer Beats* - at a former race-course in the suburb of *Riem*.

Authentic life experiences that may be communicated in real time on *Clubhouse, Facebook, Instagram, Messenger, TikTok, Twitter, YouTube, Podcasts* and *Whats-App*.

#simplymunich - Share the feeling!

Yoga in the *English Garden?*

A visit to *BMW-World?*

Planting bee-friendly shrubs in an urban-gardening hub?

Bouquets of flowers.

Fashion design. Minimalist chic.

HB - *Hofbräuhaus.*

Taste the city's gastronomic delights - from *"Viktualienmarkt Weisswurst"* to "star chef fare" from *Schubeck Am Platzl*.

And meet the locals at one of Munich's famous beer gardens ...

Paulaner am Nockherberg, Löwenbräukeller or *Gut Keferloh?*

There you can chill in good company, enjoying a beer – or two, with or without alcohol, traditional food or, indeed, *"Bring Your Own"* - from a local street market or neighbourhood store.

Vegans and vegetarians come into their own, too, with a wide and wonderful variety of restaurants and eateries.

After all, or even some of this, you will need to relax or work out at your hospitable Munich hotel.

Platzl? Bayerischer Hof?

Fit and revived you are now ready to immerse yourself in Munich's vibrant nightlife.

Gastro temples, hipster *"Lokals"*, insider discos, live-music bars, trendy nightclubs –

Dining, conversing, and dancing the night away, into the early morning hours ...

Exercise:

1. Draw up, record, and post as a PodCast a mega "Script for Millennials" for your town, city, or destination.

Chapter Title Photo: Rafting on the River Isar © Munich Convention Bureau

DIETARY REQUIREMENTS

"Seasoning does not just add flavour, it also enhances health. Herbs and spices are the only medicines which taste good."

Alfons Schubeck, *Celebrity German chef, restauranteur, and author*

Delicious food and beverages are not only etched into our taste buds but are embedded in our sense of smell and memories.

Inspiring culinary and dining experiences are a significant legacy of any Incentive Travel programme.

They are service touchpoints and intrinsic topics of discussion and debate that should always be taken seriously.

Diet is of increasing interest to consumers, as is the idea that you can do something beneficial for your health by choosing the right products, herbs, and spices.

The trend towards sustainability plays a dominant role in food choices, with the health benefits of un-processed, organic, and wholesome products having a priority.

Fresh, seasonal, and local cuisine with creative presen-tation and friendly service in atmospheric settings is an increasingly significant aspect of successful Incentive Travel, client referral and repeat business.

It is a chief consideration in terms of participant sat-isfaction, client feedback and competitive advantage - ignored by DMOs, CVBs and DMCs at their peril.

For destinations serving the *German outbound market*, for example, there are several dietary options which should be considered when seeking business and handling requests.

Vegetarianism, veganism and *diabetes* being probably three of the most relevant.

In 2020, there were over 8 million vegetarians in Ger-many (*almost 10% of the population*) and some 1.6 million Vegans (*2% of the population*).

The rapid growth of *vegan* products in Germany re-flects a rise in ethical consumerism, especially among

Millennials and Generation Z, *#FridaysForFuture* consumers.

Most Germans are, however, not giving up meat altogether, they are simply making room for more vegan and vegetarian options as part of what has been termed, a *"flexitarian"* (*Alfons Schubeck*) and *CO2-friendly* diet.

Thus, presenting opportunities for attractive, tasty, and plant-based food and beverage offerings.

A recent *Forsa* survey revealed that approximately 42 million people in Germany identify as *flexitarians* or *"part-time vegetarians."*

It is estimated that over 20% of Germans eat mostly vegetarian.

Another dietary consideration for Incentive Travel is *diabetes.*

More than 58 million EU citizens have *diabetes*; by 2045 this is forecast to rise to 66.7 million.

There were 7.5 million cases of *diabetes* last year in Germany alone (*12 % of the adult population*).

These are relevant considerations and decisive factors that should always be clarified in advance of any incentive groups travelling.

Dietary requirements are no longer *niche* concerns but *creative opportunities* that should neither be underestimated nor overlooked - irrespective of the clients or destinations concerned.

Exercise:

1. Create seasonal, organic, and CO2-friendly

- Vegetarian

- Vegan

- Flexitarian

- Diabetes

menu options for a five-course gala dinner for German Incentive Travel guests.

2. Create seasonal, organic and CO2-friendly

- Vegetarian

- Vegan

- Flexitarian

- Diabetes

menu options for a five-course awards dinner for Chinese Incentive Travel guests.

CORPORATE SOCIAL RESPONSIBILITY

Corporate Social Responsibility (CSR) in Incentive Travel involves the creation of programmes with conscious reference to their impact on the well-being of local communities, society at large and the natural environment.

Frau Anna Ran of prize-winning Berlin start-up *Wildling Shoes* states that CSR is about people, our planet and profitability. If a company is not profitable, it cannot sustainably finance CSR initiatives.

The motto being:

To give rather than to take.

The *European Commission* defines CSR as the voluntary basis for companies and corporations to bring their company and shareholder social interests and ecological values into line with their enterprise goals.

CSR means social and environmental responsibility for a company's business activities and actions.

Issues include how companies and corporations deal with business partners, employees, local communities, and human impact on the environment.

These are refined by key global developments such as Covid-19, demographic change, global warming, and sustainable use of scarce natural resources.

CSR offers great potential to the Incentive Travel sector with plenty of scope for competitive differentiation and destination leadership.

A word of caution in advance.

There is a temptation to dress CSR up as a business discipline and demand that every CSR initiative deliver business results.

That is asking too much of CSR and distracts from what its primary goal is: to align a company's social and environmental activities with its business purpose and values.

If in doing so, CSR activities mitigate risks, enhance reputation and contribute to business results, then that is highly laudable.

Co-ordinated support for CSR initiatives at the top levels of executive management is critical to success.

It is neither practical nor logical for all companies to engage in similar types of CSR activity, since CSR pro-grammes are driven by diverse economic interests and miscellaneous geographic factors.

Including the commercial, industrial, and socio-polit-ical environments in which businesses operate - and the motivations of the people who own, staff, run, and govern each company.

For example, although a manufacturing company may have excellent opportunities to reduce its environmen-tal impact, a financial services company may be hard-pressed to do so - but it may be more successful in the social and cultural sphere, with significant initiatives supporting local education and literacy efforts.

In a country lacking sufficient government funding for public health, a company's CSR funding for clean water and sanitation may be far more valuable to the local community than carbon mitigation initiatives to reduce global climate impact; while a society that en-joys effective state provision for social welfare services may place greater importance on biodiversity and eco-logical conservation.

The car insurer **AXA**, for example, is promising to

spend up to €6 million in 2021 to offset the annual carbon impact of over 650,000 cars that it insures in Ireland.

According to its own calculations, the programme will see it offsetting the equivalent of 1 million tonnes of carbon dioxide.

It is planning to do this by spending €2 million to finance the planting of 600,000 trees across 200 hectares around the country in co-operation with *The Nature Trust*.

It will also spend €4 million investing in carbon offsets involving wind, hydro and solar projects.

Best-practice organisations operate such co-ordinated and interdependent CSR programmes across an ever-changing portfolio.

Some initiatives create shared value; some create more value for society than for the company; and others are intended to create value primarily for society.

All have one thing in common though: they are aligned with company business goals, company stakeholder values, and the needs of local communities in which the companies operate.

These companies, of course, stand in stark contrast to companies that are focused solely on creating shareholder value.

Incentive Travel experts should, therefore, inform themselves in advance not only about company goals and objectives but also about the existence and nature of any *CSR policies, projects, initiatives, guidelines and directives* concerning Incentive Travel programmes and RFP bids.

Bear in mind, too, that *Sustainability and CSR Officers* are often the final voices in many organisations when it comes to ticking off all the right boxes for a travel destination or a local partner (*particularly in the larger, stock exchange-noted companies and corporations.*)

Working to eliminate Human Trafficking in Travel and Tourism - SITE and ECPAT Partnership

Human trafficking is a global issue in the travel and tourism industry. With the use of online classified ads, human trafficking has moved off the streets and behind the closed doors of hotel bedrooms.

Women and children are targeted and manipulated by traffickers who transport victims from city to city via airlines and buses. Exploiters use hotels rooms knowing that systems are not in place to identify and protect the victims. Over 80% of arrests take place in airports and hotels.

Unfortunately, very few victims are identified and fewer still receive the help and services they require. ECPAT *International* is a global network of organizations working together for the elimination of child prostitution, child pornography and the trafficking of children for sexual purposes. ECPAT has been championed in the Incentive Travel industry by Annamaria Ruffini, Past-President of SITE.

The Tourism Child-Protection Code of Conduct (The Code) - is a joint venture between the tourism private sector and ECPAT USA.

It is the only set of business principles that travel companies can implement to prevent child sex tourism and trafficking. By enacting responsible policies, members of *The Code* play an essential role in protecting children from exploitation.

QR Code: *Learn about ECPAT*

Exercise:

1. Find out what CSR policies, programmes and directives exist in your current and potential client companies post-Covid, and what you and your partners must do to be fully compliant with these.

2. Collate and list suitable environment protection programmes, climate protection initiatives and social projects for CSR support in your Incentive Travel destination.

QR Code: *AXA Carbon Offset CSR in Ireland*

CSR GUIDELINES

ISO 26000 provides guidance on how businesses and organisations can operate in a socially responsible manner. This means acting in an ethical and transparent way that contributes to the health and welfare of society at large.

QR Code: ISO 26000 – *What is CSR?*

ISO 20121 is a management system standard that has been designed to help organisations in the events industry to improve the sustainability of their event-related activities, products, and services.

QR Code: ISO 20121 - *Sustainable Events*

ISO 14001 specifies the requirements for an environmental management system that an organisation can use to enhance its environmental performance.

QR Code: ISO 14001 - *Environmental Audit*

SUSTAINABLE
INCENTIVE TRAVEL

"Actions matter more today than ever before. We can see your work, hear your words, and understand your intent."

Seth Godin, *The Practice*

Incentive Travel really can make a difference when it comes to promoting sustainable travel.

Environment protection, biodiversity, and climate change are three top concerns which will have to be intelligently and successfully addressed in the 21st century if our planet is to remain habitable.

We have no Planet B.

There are several steps which DMOs, DMCs and suppliers may undertake together with corporate Incentive Travel clients and planners to make participant experiences not only memorable but also sustainable, climate-neutral, and environment-friendly.

Promotional Materials

Paper / inks / printing methods employed – switch from paper to electronic, mobile, online, cloud and social media when possible.

Purchasing Policy

Increased interest in sustainability means our industry must be more transparent regarding suppliers.

CSR / Sustainability Officers evaluate purchasing criteria with particular focus on restaurants and catering.

Source and serve organic / regional / seasonal food & beverages where and when possible.

The quality of hotel or restaurant ties to local farming and business communities is often borne in mind before Incentive Travel contracts are signed.

Compliance with food safety and hygiene regulations is also important.

Use Of Plastics

Sir David Attenborough's "BLUE PLANET II" series for *BBC Television* was a resounding success.

It takes audiences on a journey to the deepest, darkest areas on Earth and helps us discover the wonders of the sea.

But it also illustrates the horrors that plastics are causing in our oceans.

Many of the sea creatures we love – birds, fish, turtles, and whales – die because plastic is suffocating our beaches and seas.

What can Incentive Travel and the gastronomy, accommodation, transport, and entertainment sectors do to lessen the impact of this plastic waste?

Three immediate and easily applicable measures come to mind:

1. *Reduce single-use plastics, plastic packaging and plastic containers* at breakfast, lunch, dinner, BBQ buffets, on tour coaches and cruise ships, and at *al fresco* picnics.

Avoid unnecessary use of plastics and substitute them with paper products and glass instead.

Euromonitor research states that more than one million plastic bottles are sold every minute of every day or 20,000 per second, a total of 481 billion in 2020 alone.

Less than 50% are collected for recycling and only 7% are turned into new bottles.

An estimated 8 to 12 million tonnes of plastic waste enter the oceans in a single year. This is the equivalent to dumping the contents of one refuse truck into the ocean every minute. If no action is taken, this is expected to increase to two per minute by 2030 and four per minute by 2050, when there will be - in terms of volume - more plastic in our oceans than fish.

A carelessly discarded plastic bag can break down in the sea, especially in warmer waters, but the process releases toxic chemicals that may be digested by fish and end up in the human food chain.

This process can take up to 400 years.

2. Serve, water, minerals, and other refreshments *ToGo* in *glass or aluminium multi-use bottles.*

Reduce the use of disposable plastic bottles by making it easier for trip participants to refill their water bottles.

3. Cease - when and wherever possible - serving hot beverages such as *Coffee2Go* in *plastic disposable beakers and cups.*

Energy & Water Conservation

The tourism sector has high-energy consumption - hotels in particular.

A strong positive correlation is often observed between hotel star rating and energy consumption per room.

While heating and cooling remain the main source of energy consumption, services such as heated pools, wellness spas, golf courses, and laundry, all increase energy bills.

Extra amenities (*e.g., wellness landscapes, swimming pools*), combined with changes in consumer patterns mean that modern hotels consume twice the energy of an average hotel built back in the 1970s.

Similar trends are observed in tap water consumption, too.

Consequently, many clients wishing to organise *"Green Incentives"* choose to stay at better value hotels of a lower standard or at higher range hotels that have implemented measures to monitor their energy and water consumption levels.

Employ a mix of green energy when and where possible – e.g., solar, wind, wave, hydro-electric and / or geo-thermal.

Transfer trip participants in E- or hydrogen buses and tour coaches.

Hotel Values

The hotel industry has experienced a great deal of franchise development.

Such changes to ownership models are invisible to Incentive Travel customers but they can influence the management of environmental and social matters at a local level.

CSR-minded clients often consider how hotels are monitoring these risks, considering that Incentive Travel participant satisfaction is directly correlated to hotel management and staff motivation.

A good example of recent action in this area is the *Maritim* hotel group three-pillar *"ProUmwelt-Richt-linie"* (pro-environment guideline) – which is oriented on ecological, economic, and social considerations.

Consumption data from each *Maritim* hotel is gathered and analysed in a documentation system and a *"ProUmwelt"* (pro-environment) gremium serves as a communications centre between central management and individual *Maritim* hotels.

An Example From Paris

The Best Western Opéra Liège became the first zero single-use plastic hotel in France, located in the 9th arrondissement of Paris. It worked with *Racing for the Oceans* to move from being a single-use plastic consumer to becoming a zero waste ambassador.

Together, they replaced all plastic packaging with sustainable alternatives. The hotel's 50 rooms and suites no longer feature single-use plastic, starting with wooden keycards used to access rooms. Eco-friendly amenities include laundry bags, slippers and binbags made from bamboo, plastic-free minibar products, drinking water fountain and paper *Nespresso* capsules.

Local Environment Enhancements

Plant native wildflowers, trees, and shrubs instead of foreign species as a CO_2 travel offset measure.

These support and enrich native fauna, insects, butterflies, songbirds, and honeybees.

Imagine guests wakening up to the sound of birds twittering in the morning twilight and to the flavours of locally produced honeys and jams on their breakfast bread.

In Britain and Ireland, for example, plant trees and shrubs related to, and based on, the old Celtic *Ogham* alphabet.

* * * * *

The measures listed above are not only beneficial to local environments but also deliver a major operational bonus to any Incentive Travel marketing, promotion, advertising, and public relations initiatives.

Management, staff, suppliers, and partners must be personally informed and committed from the outset for any measures to be effective and for associated messages to be credible.

Sustainable Incentive Travel is something that should not be underestimated in post-Covid times of climate change, environment conservation and enhanced competitiveness.

In terms of branding, Incentive Travel destinations should foster an image which is considered socially desirable to an even greater number and range of people – at times even fashionable, trendy and cool.

An image that will engender positive vibrations during a trip and in society-at-large.

QR Code: BLUE PLANET II

QR Code: *Maritim Hotels Environment Protection*

QR Code: OGHAM - *The Celtic Tree Alphabet*

Our challenge consists in carrying out a profitable transformation coupled with an unprecedented and sustainable Incentive Travel experience.

Exercise:

1. What measures can be taken to reduce the use of plastic packaging, containers and bottles during Incentive Travel trips?

List and keep near to hand.

2. What native trees, shrubs and meadow flowers could you plant to sustainably enhance the flora and fauna of your neighbourhood or locality?

QR Code: *How to Become a Plastic-Free Hotel*

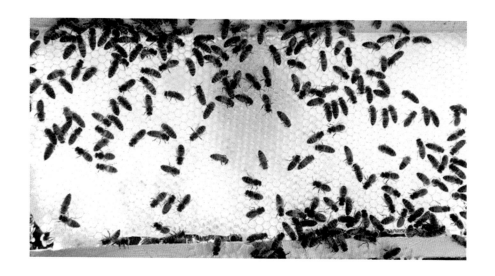

HIVESHARE AND
HONEYBEES

"Imagine freshly-produced honey from local beehives with your golden breakfast toast. Simply delicious!"

Increased annual losses in honeybee (*Apis mellifera*) colonies in Europe, North America and China are quite alarming because bees are globally important for crop pollination.

Carelessness in pesticide application has led to overuse and antibiotic resistance in honeybee parasites. Human activity is also causing the spread of pathogens that harm bee species.

The *United Nations* says that the world's bees face

multiple threats and unless something is done to halt their decline, there could be serious long-term consequences for our food supplies.

Without bees, we face a massive pollination crisis that will affect the whole planet.

"The way humanity manages or mismanages its nature-based assets, including pollinators, will in part define our collective future in the 21st century."

says *United Nations Environment Programme* executive director, Mr. Achim Steiner.

Mr. Martin Smith, President of the *British Beekeepers Association*, says:

"The BBKA is very pleased that the United Nations recognises the economic importance of managed honeybees, which make a £153 billion contribution to global food production."

"We urge increased planting of wildflower margins around agricultural fields and also stronger guidance to local authorities on increasing flowering trees and wildflower planting in towns and cities."

This is excellent advice that should be heeded by Incentive Travel planners, destination managers and accommodation providers.

"The problems facing honeybees today are complex and will not be easy to mitigate."

says bee researcher Mr. Robert Owen from the *Entomological Society of America.*

"Until people accept responsibility for the environment and acknowledge that our actions are making the future a less attractive place in which to live, we are doomed to live in a less sustainable world."

So how exactly could the Incentive Travel sector help alleviate this dramatic situation?

How could our industry assist in maintaining and supporting honeybee populations in popular Incentive Travel destinations?

One interesting idea that could be quite easily applied is the concept of **HiveShare** – whereby companies or individuals purchase shares in beehives and organic honey production.

An excellent example of HiveShare in practice is *Brookfield Farm* on the shores of beautiful Lough Derg in Co. Tipperary, Ireland.

Its owner, Ms. Ailbhe Gerrard, is not only interested in bees but is keen to make her farm a sanctuary for wildlife and insects, as well as producing excellent farm food.

Brookfield Farm Honey is a raw Irish honey gathered by bees from a large range of seasonal wildflowers and tree blossoms.

"We do very little to the honey, just extract from the natural comb and filter before putting this raw super-food into jars. Our bees are native Irish black bees, well adapted to our damp and cool climate. Bees travel up to five miles to forage for nectar and pollen. Each worker bee collects about half a teaspoon of honey in its entire lifetime, so it is very precious."

says Ms. Gerrard.

What could be nicer for Incentive Travel participants than honey from their very own honeybees and bee-hives?

HiveShare helps bees and beekeepers and offers trip participants unique insights into the cycle of the seasons on farms.

Dedicated farm visits as part of an Incentive Travel programme can also help bring this important environmental issue to life and make it far more personal and enjoyable.

Natural handmade beeswax candles and honey gift boxes are also eminently suitable as room gifts, too.

Locally produced organic honey is also to be recommended for breakfast buffets - a healthy, sustainable, and beneficial way to kick off any old day.

QR Code: *Brookfield Farm HiveShare*

Exercise:

1. Research locally produced honey in your destination and include as Room Gifts.

2. Research HiveShare opportunities in your destination that could be suitably included as environment protection and biodiversity initiatives in future Incentive Travel programmes.

BOTANIC GARDENS

"Wouldn't it be heartening to know that your Incentive Travel programme has contributed to the conservation of an endangered plant species?"

How can Incentive Travel interact positively with nature and support conservation efforts - other than visiting beautiful scenery and hosting activities and outdoor receptions in stunning natural settings?

Could *Botanic Gardens* provide positive impulses post-Covid for Incentive Travel planners and trip participants?

A recent *University of Cambridge* study found out that the world's botanic gardens contain about a third of all known plants and help protect 40% of endangered species.

Scientists say that with one in five of the world's plants on the brink of extinction, botanic collections hold the key to saving rare plant life.

In the light of this, wouldn't it be fantastic if the world's botanic gardens and natural scientists received increased support from the Incentive Travel sector - making sustainable contributions both to participant experiences and to *Life on Earth*?

In the first detailed study of plants grown in botanic gardens, the *University of Cambridge* recorded more than 100,000 species.

"This is the first time that we have carried out a global assessment to look at the wide range of plants grown, managed and conserved in botanic gardens."

says Dr. Paul Smith, Secretary General of the global charity *Botanic Gardens Conservation International* - the world's largest plant conservation network.

"For the first time we know what we have and, perhaps more importantly, what is missing from botanic gardens."

Some 500 million people visit botanic gardens every year. As well as being popular tourist attractions, they are centres of learning and education, conducting valuable research and conservation work.

The *University of Cambridge* study, published in the journal *Nature Plants*, identified gaps in the botanic collections of more than 1,000 institutions.

Many botanic gardens are in the Northern Hemisphere where tropical species are harder to maintain as they need to be grown in heated glasshouses.

Tropical plants are best grown in their country of origin, but there are far fewer facilities in the Southern Hemisphere.

Only 10% of global collections are dedicated to threatened species, suggesting botanic gardens could do more to preserve some of the world's most vulnerable plants.

Dr. Samuel Brockington of the *University of Cambridge* is a curator at the university's botanic garden and co-researcher of the study.

He says that the global network of botanic gardens is the best hope for saving some of the world's most endangered plants.

"Currently, an estimated one-fifth of plant diversity is under threat, yet there is no technical reason why any plant species should become extinct. If we do not conserve our plant diversity, humanity will struggle to solve the global challenges of food and fuel security, environmental degradation, and climate change."

Botanic Gardens present, therefore, many excellent opportunities for Incentive Travel planners, beneficiaries / qualifiers, CVBs, DMOs and DMCs alike to actively assist and support this valuable work.

This can be easily incorporated into tour planning, event organisation, trip delivery, financial sponsorship, voluntary contributions, CSR, industry awareness and public advocacy measures.

And these are fantastic stories waiting to be told.

QR Code: *Botanic Gardens Conservation International*

Exercise:

1. How could you assist Botanic Gardens to preserve some of the world's most vulnerable plants by including them in your Incentive Travel planning, trip delivery, financial sponsorship, voluntary contributions,

CSR support, industry awareness and public advocacy initiatives?

2. Which is your favourite Botanic Garden in the whole wide world and why?

STORYTELLING

"We need to replace our standard authority, logic and proof storylines with dramatic tales filled with empathy, suspense and surprise to captivate low-attention audiences in our present Age of Interruption."

Dr. James McCabe, *The Story Doctor*

When marketing Incentive Travel destinations we consider what we have to offer and what we intend to present to local, regional, and international markets.

We examine distribution chains, contact linkages and influencer networks.

Attentively listening to and incorporating feedback from clients, agencies, carriers, guides, accommodation, venues, and restaurants is all an important part of this process.

But what stories do we as Incentive Travel destination marketers want to tell Incentive Travel planners & beneficiaries / qualifiers post-Covid - before, during and after their visits?

In today's social media marketing jargon - which content do we wish to present, how, where and when?

And are we telling the right and appropriate tales?

If nobody has ever heard of us - of where we are at, and of where we are planning to go - then nobody will ever be aware of us, pay any attention to us or do any business with us.

So, which *"Influencers"* and actors can we get on board to enhance and help us in our storytelling efforts?

And which audacious stories will we tell when our current tales have already been told?

Blogger Jeff Hurt published an article on *"Event Profis as Content Strategists and as Curators"*.

In it he says that:

"It is critical for meeting professionals to create conference experiences that have purpose, are contextual and spur discussion".

Hurt suggests that events organisers might follow in the footsteps of museum curators in that they should approach content as a medium that needs to be strategically selected and carefully placed to engage the audience in question, convey a message and inspire action.

This is sound advice and got me thinking about the Incentive Travel sector, which has plenty in common not only with museum curators, but also with theatre directors and movie producers - with respect to their ways of thinking and methods of approach.

Content, presentations, and locations should, as Hurt suggests, be juxtaposed against one another to create meaning, spur engagement, generate excitement and deliver enjoyable and rewarding experiences once again.

Incentive Travel planners' goals, for example, concerning content and location selection could involve:

1. Creating narrative stories and themes that can be followed through from the initial announcement to the conclusion of an Incentive Travel programme.

2. Creating awareness and desire by carefully distilling key messages in the light of what has been learnt from engaging with trip participants and hearing what they have to say.

3. Evoking imaginative responses from beneficiaries, qualifiers and participants - prior to, during and after the trip.

4. Communicating key messages and stories in all

manners, media, and forms.

5. Inspiring storytelling and interpersonal exchange in fun, relaxing and interactive contexts, and environ-ments.

The object of the lesson being to:

Move from WHAT you are doing now to WHY you are doing it, WHAT you are planning to do and WHY, and WHY in future Incentive Travel clients should WANT to do it with you.

Now that is some story to tell, so practice till you are perfect!

And while you are about it, please also consider Peter Turley's neat **60-30-10** '*Pitch Perfect*' formula for sales pitches:

- 60% of what you present should be about your cli-ents' needs (*the tasks and challenges at hand*).

- 30% should be about your event concept and story-line (*the Incentive Travel solutions you propose*) and only

- 10% should be about YOU (*the creative local experts and problem solvers*).

Too many people spend a lot of their and other people's time talking about themselves and about what wonderful companies and destinations they rep-resent.

So, maybe it's high time to turn these conversations on their heads, and in the words of the renowned Irish retail entrepreneur, Feargal Quinn - *"Crown the Customer"* instead.

Exercise:

1. What's Your Story?

*2. Write down your **60-30-10** sales pitch and present it live.*

LANGUAGE AND IMAGES

"Mirabile dictu!"

Vergil, 'Aeneid' ("Wonderful to relate!")

"A picture paints a thousand words; a video paints a thousand pictures."

Peter Turley, Blood, Sweat and Sales

When working with international Incentive Travel planners it is important to ensure that most, if not all, of your Incentive Travel information, websites and materials are in the relevant client language - English at the very least.

Your offers should feature a clear simple structure with precise and transparent language.

Communication is, after all, about the transfer of information.

Offers should include professional translation of details and information if required by customers, along with clearly explained components, optional extras, terms and conditions, terms of payment and cancellations policy.

Language guides and service personnel are also to be highly recommended.

Food & Beverage menus to be translated by a native speaker if requested.

This should all be backed up by quality high-resolution photographic images and videos (*e.g., YouTube/ Vimeo*) that enhance and support emotional messages.

A great thing about Incentive Travel is that powerful images and videos speak a language all of their own and can close a sale for RFP bids while creating latent desire and positive feelings on the part of potential beneficiaries / qualifiers.

Photos, videos and written offers should be accompanied by detailed descriptions suitable for inclusion in client presentations, print materials, news releases, and web landing-pages - along with easily understood catchwords and phrases.

Always bear in mind that attention spans are declining, and people are growing increasingly impatient and more demanding as communications technology develops.

The potentially infinite scrolls of social media news feeds and endless streams of content force people to filter out most messages as "*White Noise*", i.e., random content and messages with no immediate attraction, relevance or personal appeal.

We skim articles and skip posts.

That is why so-called *"Dense Content"* is now the key to effective Incentive Travel storytelling, we must ensure that every picture, every video, every line, and every single word counts.

And think carefully, too, about how you employ colours and colour tones to relay different messages and moods - for every colour conveys a signal and an emotion.

And these can vary according to gender, age, culture, geography and background, too.

A fun and useful exercise is to **"Say it in a Tweet"** – condensing your core messages / USPs / UVPs to 280 characters - with an eye-catching photo or two to tease, and a web landing-page for further information, videos, .pdfs, and or / calls-to-action.

And - finally - please pay special attention to grammar,

punctuation, tone, and syntax and ensure that everything you produce is proof-read by a native-speaking colleague before it is finally delivered to clients, beneficiaries / qualifiers, trip participants and service suppliers.

Exercise:

1. "Say it in a Tweet" - summarize your destination, city, and or company USPs / UVPs in 280 characters (including a landing-page link for further information / video / .pdf flyer / brochure download).

To this, you can add an eye-catching high-resolution .jpeg photograph, photo collage, company logo and / or animated .gif.

NETWORKING

"Networking is not about selling but about building relationships which will ultimately lead to new sales opportunities."

Alex Drew, *The Business Expert*

Tony Hsieh states in his bestselling book, *"Delivering Happiness – A Path to Passion, Profits and Purpose"*, that he really disliked *"business networking"* events.

He says that the goal of most of the events he ever attended was to walk around and find people to trade business cards with, in the hope of meeting someone who could help him in business.

In exchange, he might also be able to help that person out in return.

He advises us to stop trying to *"network"* in the traditional sense of the term and to try and grow the number and depth of our personal friendships - where friendship itself is its own ultimate reward.

Sounds reasonable?

Tony Hsieh is convinced from his experience that the more diverse friendships are, the more likely we will derive both personal and business benefits from these down the line.

Makes sense?

I remember when I was young that my parents used to attend *"Socials"*.

These were none other than networking events but without the business cards.

The foreground emphasis was on the social, but such gatherings solidified a support structure that transcended any purely business aspects.

Many of us were involved pre-Covid in organising and attending *"business-to-business networking events"* that had a social character.

Some of our best and longest-standing business relationships were established during the social as opposed to the more formal business meetings at these events.

Often in the hotel bar afterwards - or, for example,

during a coach tour through the spectacular, terraced, and verdant mountain landscapes on the island of *Madeira*.

So, rather than talking about B2B networking, maybe post-Covid we should be returning to the concept of face-to-face social business occasions where participants can simply catch-up and get to know each other better.

Where time is taken to rekindle old friendships, strengthen existing bonds and establish new relationships without having to immediately *Link-In*.

Future Incentive Travel events could be promoted as social business occasions whereby the strictly business also makes way for a *"familial"* community atmosphere - such as that experienced by SITE members at *SITE Global* and *SITE Chapter* events.

Who knows, who we will meet - or be introduced to next, exchange stories with, end up helping and doing quality business with?

As Ted Rubin (*Return on Relationship*), says:

"A network gives you reach. A community gives you power."

It is also important to be clear about the *typus* of Incentive Travel clients and suppliers we hope to meet at such networking events.

And they, too, should be hopefully aware of who we

are - and of all the wonderful things we could do to assist them.

That way we leave less scope to serendipity and more space to providence.

This is not only a change in paradigm and terminology, but also a call to reflect upon and engage in further personal and business transformation.

Imagine what this could do for your confidence and for your ability to get to the right conversation the next time you enter a networking space.

Creating safe and comfortable networking spaces post-Covid poses its own challenges, but if any branch manages to come up with fitting and robust solutions to future networking requirements, it will be ours.

As Tony Hsieh says at the end of his book, you will not know exactly what the benefits will be, but if the friendships (*and potential business contacts*) are genuine, those benefits will indeed magically appear.

Giving us fitting cause for cautious optimism and future reward.

QR Code: *SITE Global Networking Events*

Exercise:

Close your eyes.

1. Imagine what your ideal networking space looks and feels like?

2. What factors contribute to making you feel comfortable and safe there?

TRADE FAIR ETIQUETTE

"Don't you feel exhausted but really good after exciting and productive days at ITB Berlin or IMEX Frankfurt?"

Most leading international travel trade fairs and MICE exhibitions were cancelled because of Covid-19 - *ITB Berlin* and *IMEX Frankfurt* being two very good examples.

What follows is an article I wrote almost a decade ago about traditional trade fair etiquette in Germany.

After reading, it will be interesting for you to contemplate how personal B2B interaction and etiquette will develop post-Covid?

How much physical distancing will be required at future events and exhibitions?

And indeed, how many of the tips listed below will continue to apply in conjunction with post-Covid health & safety protocols?

The *Wall Street Journal* reckons that Covid and its variants are here to stay for quite some time so we are all going to have to learn to live and work with them.

So, how will hosted-buyer programmes run when colleagues might no longer be willing or permitted to fly - let alone transferred by tour coaches and ushered around exhibition halls to attend tightly packed presentations and appointments on exhibitor stands, attend gala dinners and live networking events?

What are the implications for hall layout, booth design and stand catering?

Is there potential for hybrid formats?

Will these prove sustainable in the long run in the light of basic human requirements to communicate and interact with other human beings *in situ*?

ORIGINAL BLOG ARTICLE

When I was a young lad of nine, we had an already dated Primary School textbook titled, *"Courtesy for Boys and Girls"*.

This dealt with subjects such as deportment in public and behaviour at table.

Even back then - in 1969 - it was considered somewhat of an *"Edwardian"* anachronism in the brave world of the *"New Curriculum"*.

So, it was abandoned soon after that.

A great pity - some would say.

Nowadays, textbooks and courses on social and business *etiquette* for children and adults are booming once again.

"Knigge" is a very good example from Germany.

This got me thinking about business *etiquette* as it applies to colleagues from English-speaking countries either visiting or exhibiting at trade exhibitions in Germany.

The following are some tips which may enhance your B2B trade exhibition attendance, saving you time, and ensuring that your efforts are not only effective - but also productive.

Many still apply in other countries, too.

Timing is everything: write to your clients / potential clients in advance of an exhibition informing them of your stand presence if you are an exhibitor, or of your intention to attend, and desire for an appointment if you are a trade visitor.

Enclose targeted information on your new products, services, offers and stand location.

But please don't overload.

Differentiate in scope, content, and form between established, new, and potential *contacts*.

In the case of *new or desired contacts* - please ensure you research their companies and *LinkedIn* biographies and that you possess the correct names, titles, positions, and degrees of decision-making responsibility for the persons you wish to meet.

Follow up by phone if necessary if you have not received a reply within a fortnight.

Make use of the first day of the exhibition and of any optional seminar / networking events to make additional *business appointments*.

The final day of the exhibition is usually a good bet for making *ad hoc* appointments and connections, since appointment schedules are often less crowded.

Clarify the exact date, time, location, and duration of *meetings* – whether on-stand or off.

Rehearse your *sales pitch* in advance.

Anticipate *questions* and formulate *answers*.

Keep to the agreed appointment time – *punctuality* is a virtue in Germany and elsewhere.

If, for some reason or other, the appointment cannot be maintained, then please inform your contact in advance to allow for sufficient time to cancel or re-arrange.

If the meeting is on your exhibition stand or booth, then please make sure that you offer hospitality / re-freshments (*coffee, mineral water, soft drinks*).

Refrain from using *plastic utensils* and ensure that the necessary *table / seating* spaces are available and that you remain undisturbed for the duration of the meet-ing.

Make sure all participants understand the *subject mat-ter of the meeting*, so come prepared – ask ques-tions and have answers to potential questions (*rates, availability, venues, terms and conditions*) at the ready (*e.g., on your mobile phone, laptop, diary or tablet computer*).

Make sure you also have a sufficient supply of personal business cards and / or promotional material (*if re-quired*) to hand.

Send all necessary *information and support materials* in the week following the exhibition - or when specific-ally requested to do so by a client / prospective client. By e-mail if possible.

This saves either carrying bulky bags or taking up valu-able stand space with storage, and prevents material being thrown away and / or lost after the show - and it also lightens your partners' load.

Duration of appointment: aim for *10 minutes* at the exhibition.

This can always be extended or moved off-exhibition if your appointment so desires.

If not, you will not have exceeded your welcome and you will make a good impression.

Turn your *mobile / cell phone* off during the course of your meeting.

Always give your full attention and don't be diverted by what is happening all around you.

In addressing strangers or business partners, Germans mostly use the formal mode of address (*Sie in German / Vous in French*), i.e., surnames and not first names.

The informal mode of address (*Du in German / Tu in French*) is rarely used in business transactions.

First names and the *Du / Tu* forms are subsequently used upon invitation only. This being a sign of familiarity, friendship and trust.

Follow-up all requests and proposals on time and deliver products and services as agreed.

Tip for *E-Mail* correspondence: write texts in full as you would speak as a matter of courtesy, avoid abbreviations, keep content formal, short and to the point.

Provide full contact details.

Exercise:

1. Plan and Design a detailed Briefing Document for an exhibition stand builder for a

- 20 square metre

- 40 square metre

- 80 square metre

Covid-compliant MICE international trade exhibition stand for your company or destination.

2. What is different this time round compared to when you last exhibited pre-Covid?

3. How are you going to manage hosted buyer groups and trade visitor appointments post-Covid?

DIGITAL DETOX

"Digital detox" is an attempt to untether individuals from obsessively checking their mobile phones.

It is an attempt to forcibly unleash people from the global addiction of compulsively taking photos, checking messages, updating social media channels, and replying to e-mails, texts, and messages when on holiday or participating in business events.

It is an issue that the *Ayana Resort* on Bali, for example, has addressed by limiting the use of smartphones and mobile devices by their *River Pool* in a bid to encourage guests to absorb their surroundings rather than stare at a screen.

Guests should enjoy a swim in the sea, read a book,

catch up with family and friends by writing postcards, or just simply relax in and enjoy the moment.

The phenomenon of being unable to switch off, or be parted from your mobile phone, has been given a new name: *nomophobia* - sometimes described as the "21st *century disease"*.

Social media use has been linked to depression, particularly among young people and Millennials.

A recent survey of American holidaymakers by *OnePoll* found that more than 20 % said they checked their smartphones once per hour during their most recent holiday, while about 14 % said they checked it twice per hour. Nearly 8 % said they checked it more than 20 times per hour.

In a *Deloitte* survey in Britain in 2017, 38 % of adults said they thought they were using their smartphones far too much.

Vienna's tourist board recently unveiled a campaign titled, *"Unhashtag Vienna"* - encouraging visitors to get off social media and enjoy the city behind the pictures!

Its provocative tagline:

See Vienna. Not #Vienna.

The *Vienna Tourist Board* wants visitors and MICE event participants to enjoy the moment and the city behind the pictures – instead of documenting it on so-cial media.

The start of the campaign was marked by a *"See Klimt. Not #Klimt."* event where Gustav Klimt's famous painting, *Kiss in the Belvedere Palace*, was swapped with a replica and covered with a red hashtag, with visitors' reactions captured on film.

As a result of this publicity, there has been a surge of interest in so-called *"Digital Detox Holidays"*.

This growing trend for switching off and embracing *"digital detox"* relaxation and momentary awareness enhancement could be imaginatively and quite easily adopted and marketed by the Incentive Travel sector post-Covid.

Opportunities are plenty and creativity is by no means short in supply.

QR Code: *"See Vienna. Not #Vienna."*

(*YouTube* video)

Exercise:

1. Create a Digital Detox tagline and advertising campaign for your Incentive Travel destination.

SLOWING DOWN

Incentive Travel is popular because it is good for social cohesion, team spirit and general well-being – as well as being excellent value for money.

The trend towards *"slowing-down"* programmes pre-Covid was not about doing everything at a snail's pace but about seeking to do everything at the right speed, savouring the hours and minutes in a destination rather than just counting them, doing everything as well as possible, instead of as fast as possible.

This mindset is probably more significant today than ever before as our industry gets back onto its feet and starts moving once again.

Milan Kundera in his novel „*Slowness*" (1995), states

that:

"The degree of slowness is directionally proportional to the intensity of memory. The degree of speed is directionally proportional to the intensity of forgetting."

The advantages of slowing Incentive Travel down are many.

These include meeting people and experiencing the attractions of a destination closer-up, how the locals live, work and play, what the history, archaeology, landscape, music, art and culture is all about.

Immersion as opposed to fleeting glances - memorable interactions and living experiences as opposed to ticking off wish lists and visitor sights - becoming part of the scenery as opposed to just passing through it.

If every second of a programme is pre-scheduled, then there is little time left for unexpected encounters or for allowing trip participants time to think about what they have seen or what they have experienced.

Slow or Immersive Incentive Travel as opposed to packed and stressful *"run off your feet"* trips are more economical and environment-friendly, too, as participants experience possibilities to relax and explore by foot, by horse-carriage, by boat, by public transport, and by bicycle.

(e.g., the memorable SITE European Conference 2000 *in Bruges, Belgium; the* SITE EMEA Forum 2012 *in Ber-*

lin; and SITE Germany Get-Togethers at ITB Berlin).

Trip participants, with the assistance of qualified local guides, start talking to and interacting with other people in shops, cafés, and pubs, at festivals and at home. Tasting chocolate and drinking coffee.

They attend cookery courses, learn to bake bread, have a laugh, post photographs or paint watercolours; see lambs being born, sheep being shorn, cows being milked, or racehorses being groomed ... taking time out to allow things happen at their own pace and for newly gained impressions to slowly sink in.

One of *The Eagles* greatest hits - *Take it Easy* - could be taken as a suitable anthem for this relaxing philosophy of "*Slow Incentive Travel*".

"The Eagles Generation" are now entering a phase in their lives where they are being advised by doctors to slow down, take exercise, travel, and enjoy life – they are becoming smart and active seniors even if they do not consider or feel themselves to be such.

The challenge for destinations and for DMCs post-Covid is to adapt and re-adjust traditional Incentive Travel offerings to a plethora of changing demographics, health & safety considerations, fashions and trends, client wishes and trip participant age-group requirements.

While at the same time attracting, motivating, and catering for both traditional and new generations of In-centive Travel clients, beneficiaries and qualifiers.

So, it is up to you to come up with imaginative answers to these challenges, slowly but surely, because the world is still very much your oyster.

Exercise:

1. *Plan an afternoon "Slow Incentive Travel" immersive tour experience of your nearest town or city for a 40-strong party of multi-generation participants of diverse genders, cultures and backgrounds.*

2. *Create a #Hashtag slogan for this event which trip participants can use when sharing photos and posts on social media (i.e., only if it is not a "Digital Detox" tour right from the outset.)*

QR Code: *"Take it Easy" (YouTube video)*

ETHICS

"What are they but the dreams of the young heart?"

Mr. Merryman in Goethe's *Faust - Prelude at the Theatre*

Incentive Travel in Germany and in the USA was hit over a decade ago not only by global banking crises, but by press revelations of rather unethical behaviour during a number of international Incentive Travel programmes.

The insurance corporations and automobile manufacturers in question have, in the meantime, publicly seen the light.

They have introduced stringent ethical and procurement guidelines for dealer and broker incentives while continuing to regard Incentive Travel as a legitimate means of increasing sales, rewarding, and recognising performance, and maintaining seller / distributor loyalty.

So, too, have companies who were not actually involved with the published scandals but who were nonetheless tarnished by the same brush.

The public at large, however, was not presented with a positive image of Incentive Travel. Nor were they impressed by what they saw, i.e., the fact that the programmes in question were financed by their insurance premiums and set off against corporation tax liability.

Corporate users from other sectors - where independent brokers also play a major role - dived for cover in the light of all this publicity, giving rise to an impression that Incentive Travel was a "*cloak and dagger*" operation, with a *"Geschmäckle"* (bad taste in one's mouth) - something only to be aired behind closed doors.

If this was not bad enough, a new and more worrying twist to the story came in the form of a wake-up call for the Incentive Travel industry.

In an article published in September 2012 in the *"Frankfurter Rundschau"* a renowned German psychologist questioned the whole legitimacy of reward, recognition, and motivation programmes.

She stated that such programmes were simply beneath human dignity. It was immoral that only a top few were being constantly recognized and rewarded.

The unrewarded majority were the foundation of corporate and economic success because they performed well and were in little need of any additional motivation.

The concept of having to motivate people with *"the winner takes it all"* incentives was to be considered intrinsically and morally degrading.

In *Quo Vadis?* I explored the beneficiaries / qualifiers and goals of future Incentive Travel.

What may be added to this - in the light of the ethical issues raised in Germany and in the USA - is not just an ethical and publicly acceptable approach to what we may call the traditional *"Alpha Male Winner Takes It All"* qualifiers - but also a more inclusive approach for the broader-based, and frequently forgotten, *"Beta Wave"* majority.

Incentive Travel destinations cannot afford to let such sleeping dogs lie. An image publicly tarnished in two of the world's largest economies is highly relevant, and of existential value for everybody involved in our industry.

Our task is to continually address such issues openly before they arise and raise their ugly heads once again.

While at the same time, discovering new ways of including and serving far more diverse and inclusive

"*Beta Wave*" beneficiaries in an ethical manner.

And publish positive results for all and sundry to read and to see.

Who knows, maybe this will witness Incentive Travel partners engaging in fabulous new fields of CSR service, fair recognition, and justifiable reward.

In 2023, SITE celebrates 50 years.

No mean feat it must be said. SITE as an organisation and industry voice has been influential over past five decades in spreading the word about the benefits of Incentive Travel - from the USA to almost every corner of the globe.

SITE members' creativity in programme conception and in successful trip delivery has positively influenced the broader meetings, conferences, and live events sectors, so much so that we now speak of a global '*MICE industry*'.

SITE membership, for those not in the know, is based on members signing up to and agreeing to abide by a **SITE Code of Ethics** - an excellent model and point of reference for anyone wishing to address this important subject in a serious and sustainable manner.

QR Code: *SITE Code of Ethics*

Exercise:

1. Reflect upon and discuss ethical considerations of Incentive Travel post-Covid.

2. How, where, when and for whom should you publish details of successfully run Incentive Travel programmes?

PERFECT FAM TRIPS

"What would it mean to your clients and stakeholders if you were considered a global authority in the conception and delivery of perfectly-run fam trips?"

Familiarisation - or fam - trips are a significant component of destination marketing in the Incentive Travel sector.

Factors such as clients, branch, beneficiaries, qualifiers, partners, timing, themes, concept, content, invitations, communications, trip-delivery, and participant follow-up have all to be considered, planned, and addressed in detail.

Unlike classic destination marketing, what attracts a global Incentive Travel planner may not be a famous visitor icon, but a little-known, though highly suitable local attraction.

I recommend organising market-specific, Covid-compliant, and small immersive trips with an efficiently delivered programme geared specifically to fam trip participants' work schedules and client requirements.

Every fam trip component should provide clear answers to three basic questions:

- *Who are we?*

- *What can we offer?*

- *What value derives for the client?*

While *invitations* may be of a teaser or creative nature, they should feature for compliance and fiscal reasons a short paragraph listing services that will be provided free-of-charge such as flights, accommodation, and meals.

Incentive Travel planners also want to see in advance which destination *stakeholders* are involved to make their decision easier and / or to have their participation signed off by superiors.

As part of the *registration process*, feel free to ask potential fam trip participants about any specific information they would like to receive during the trip and any special themes which might be of interest to them.

Fam trip participants are not only your "*agents*", they

are also your industry multipliers and opinion-formers. Their *advance feedback* is extremely valuable in tweaking what you intend to offer and to present.

Please bear in mind that when a planner accepts a fam trip invitation they re-arrange their work schedule appropriately, especially as the trip may take up a considerable part of their working week or weekend.

They accept and register in good faith and expect you to delivery what you promise.

Plan events out of high-season (*March to June; September to early-November*) and out of school and public holidays (*depending on the country and / or Federal State*).

Confirmations to fam trip participants should contain day-by-day programme timing, including full contact information details for hotel accommodation used along with an emergency contact number.

Use of *subtle headings* and *short evocative syntax* should leave plenty of room for exclamation and surprise during the trip itself.

Germans, for example, like to experience fam trips as their clients would. Your trip is, therefore, not a dress-rehearsal and not some abstract entity.

It is the real thing.

So, make your guests welcome and comfortable from the outset.

Draw upon their *curiosity* and willingness to learn. Encourage their active participation and *listen* to their considered criticism and *record* their spontaneous feedback.

This means you must choose your concept and themes, partners and locations, your accompanying staff, your coach drivers, and your tour guides very carefully.

They all must be *briefed in advance* and allowed to input ideas and suggestions of their own.

You may even include an *"Informal get-together"* over local food and entertainment on the first evening where all the trip's stakeholders are present.

Always remember that people and relationships are what the Incentive Travel industry is all about.

German planners will, for example, seek perfect logistics and adequate capacities for what their business requires - timed to provide a sense of what they are all about but neither hectic nor rushed.

They lay special emphasis upon efficient and friendly service; cleanliness and no obvious wear and tear; creativity and surprise; novelty in detail and - above all - a competent, hospitable, and professional approach.

Remember that your fam trip is *"live"* and that you have only one chance to impress!

Fam trip participants can never guarantee that they

will use the specific hotels where they stay nor the locations and venues they visit.

Many of today's Incentive Travel programmes have strict client procurement, hygiene, and compliance guidelines. So, decisions will depend on who is doing the buying.

Stakeholders *(DMCs, DMOs, CVBs, hotels, restaurants, activity venues or AV suppliers, entertainers, airlines, cruise, coach, or rail transport companies)* should concentrate on telling their stories and explaining exactly what they do and what they can offer.

They should highlight elements such as F & B, entertainment, logistical and communications mastery, and how they can go that extra mile in becoming a *"Stage"* where fam trip participants can imagine their Incentive Travel programmes being rehearsed and acted out.

That way your stakeholders will ensure a unique, motivating, and memorable experience, proving themselves to be Incentive Travel professionals and reliable hosts.

People with whom your fam trip participants would really like to do business with.

At the end of the final day, you should present a post-breakfast or pre-lunch 15 - 20-minute *trip summary* with AV back-up: who they met, what they experienced and how all this could help them find solutions to their company and / or client needs.

Preferably in a simple but unusual setting. This will be very much appreciated. Feedback received at this point is also most valuable.

It is worth bearing in mind, too, that your fam trip participants often fly with airlines who can handle and service Incentive Travel requirements.

Talk to your airline partners about upgrades and passes for business lounges.

This is all part and parcel of selling your destination. For first and last impressions usually begin and end at airports!

Exercise:

1. *Conceive an unforgettable client fam trip for your Incentive Travel destination post-Covid.*

2. *What is new regarding logistics and trip delivery?*

3. *What remains the same?*

4. *What are the principal challenges?*

5. *What are your creative solutions?*

GUIDES, DRIVERS & SERVICE PERSONNEL

"Do you think your clients would feel eternally grateful to you if you could mesmerize their trip participants with unforgettable tour guides?"

Tour guides, coach drivers, reception staff and service personnel are important channels of communication, storytellers, and nodes of interaction for the Incentive Travel sector.

Their motivation and professionalism in relaying information and in delivering quality service can influence perceptions of a destination's suitability and eligibility.

They can tell your stories; help establish the right atmosphere, and add authenticity to the overall partici-pant experience.

To use modern marketing terminology, they are a branding opportunity and a branded experience, i.e., your destination's calling cards.

Trained and motivated guides, tour coach chauffeurs, and hotel / restaurant / venue service personnel are a sure guarantee for well-received and safe Incentive Travel.

Investment here is a sound investment in a destin-ation's or Incentive Travel programme's success.

Exercise:

1. Review investment in training, insurance, pay and conditions for Incentive Travel tour guides in either your own - or a chosen destination. Is there room for improvement?

QR Code: WFTGA - *World Federation of Tourist Guide Associations*

WHY YOU?

"Wouldn't it be just brilliant if your colleagues and peers came to consider you as 'The Super Grey Beard' of Incentive Travel?"

The following is an enjoyable and enlightening exercise which you can carry out with your colleagues and friends.

Prepare a concise "3W Sales Pitch".

Select simple ideas which focus listeners' attention - credible ideas and stories which are easy to understand and to remember, and which strike an emotional chord.

Above all ideas, stories, or suggestions which listeners feel they will be able to act upon.

Why your Incentive Travel destination?

Why your city / region / locality?

Why your company?

In other words, what is it exactly that makes you different to - and stand out from your competitors?

What is your Unique Value Proposition?

This, of course, is easier said than done, but I find that it is an effective exercise, a fun way to focus the mind and to achieve concrete business results - the ultimate object of which could be formulated for Incentive Travel destinations as follows:

$$UX = E \times (TD1 + TD2)$$

Incentive Travel User Experience (UX) equals the emotions (E) generated (x) by trip design / context (TD1) and trip delivery / functionality (TD2).

You can now think about this *conundrum* while listening to Ireland's 1992 *Eurovision Song Contest* winning entry, *"Why me"*, written by *Mr. Eurovision* himself, Johnny Logan, and performed by Linda Martin.

1992 was also the year that Patrick Delaney was SITE President - the first ever European to hold that prestigious office.

QR Code: *"Why me" (YouTube video)*

TIPS FOR DESTINATIONS

"Do you think it's at all possible to summarize this little book in two dozen Tips and a handy mathematical formula?"

§ 1. Develop an **Incentive Travel Business Case** for why companies and organisations should hold their Incentive Travel events in your destination.

§ 2. Draw up a list **industrial, commercial, scientific** and other contacts who could help provide clients not just with local expertise but also with imaginative and branch-appropriate settings for their Incentive Travel programmes.

§ 3. When looking for potential **business drivers** of

corporate Incentive Travel, stay focused on senior management's concerns.

§ 4. Monitor **Incentive Travel agencies** (*national and international*) on a regular basis to keep track of customer service requirements and trip delivery expectations.

§ 5. Identify where and how you may obtain **Preferred Partner Status** with incentive agencies.

§ 6. Develop a catalogue of key arguments for corporate Procurement and **CSR / Sustainability Officers**.

§ 7. Create a concise list of your destination's **USPs** and **UVPs**.

$ 8. List insider tips for **"hip"** and **unusual venues**, affordable **hotels** with attractive design and friendly ambience - and **"in" pubs** and **restaurants**.

§ 9. List programme delivery possibilities in the **natural and rural environs** of your destination.

§ 10. Ensure **value for money, friendly hospitality**, and a **safe, comfortable atmosphere** always.

§ 11. Record and catalogue **Case Studies** to generate

training materials, trade press coverage, online publicity, and market demand.

§ 12. Reflect on how to create and deliver self-defining and diverse Incentive Travel experiences that meet the requirements and needs of **multiple generations, positions,** and **genders**. Draw up a mega *"Script for Millennials"*.

§ 13. Reflect on how to create Incentive Travel that **inspires and connects** trip participants from the very first minute, has purpose, is contextual and spurs discussion.

§ 14. See how you can provide for the **inclusion of family members** and **partners**.

§ 15. Explore possibilities for the inclusion of **CSR elements** with conscious reference to their impact on the well-being of local communities and the natural environment – take a lead from acknowledged best-practice.

§ 16. **#PBT** - Reduce single-use **Plastics**, support HiveShare and **HoneyBees**, plant wildflowers and native **Trees.**

§ 17. Draw up a list of best practices and reliable partners for immersive **Information Tours & Fam Trips**.

§ 18. Ensure that you work with professional **Incentive Travel guides, transport providers** and **coach drivers** who are highly motivated, fully briefed, properly trained and adequately insured and compensated.

§ 19. Ensure that all your information, websites, social media and print materials are in the **relevant syntax, tone, and language** for the clients and customers you are doing business with.

§ 20 ***"Say it in a Tweet"*** – condense your core message / USP / UVP to 280 characters ... with a photo to tease and landing-page link for further information, video, and or / call-to-action.

§ 21. Prepare a concise "***3W Sales Pitch***" to be ready for e.g., *IMEX Frankfurt, IMEX America* and *IBTM World*.

§ 22. Organise regular DMC, DMO, and CVB **Partner Training Seminars** together with external coaches and moderators.

§ 23. Update and disseminate **Health & Safety Protocols** in real-time.

§ 24. Participate in Incentive Travel industry conferences and certification, such as SITE's **CITP: Certified Incentive Travel Professional** qualification programme.

Finally, a nifty "*mathematical*" formula for successful and memorable Incentive Travel programmes is as follows: **UX = E x (TD1 + TD2)**

Incentive Travel User Experience (UX) equals the emotions (E) generated (x) by trip design / context (TD1) and trip delivery / functionality (TD2).

BRIGHT NEW
WONDERFUL LIVES

Dynamic strength exalted

Energetic goals

Creative charges

Positive poles

Brimming capacities

Thoughts of planning

And moulding deep spaces

Into arenas for living

Bright new wonderful lives

Poem published in

"FOOTSTEPS - Poetry & Prose 1987 - 2021"

by

PATRICK PATRIDGE

CONCLUDING REMARKS

"Isn't enthusiasm for what we do simply just wonderful and amazing?"

Productivity, passion, resilience, and innovation are essential factors in human progress and in business success.

Well-trained and highly motivated people are what power innovation, and it is real people who motivate other people.

Human motivation is highly influenced by the recognition, interest, and sympathy of other individuals.

This motivation is generated by positive interpersonal relationships that are balanced with care, attention, empathy, and sound leadership.

Incentive Travel is a global management tool that can assist post-Covid, because it is a tried-and-trusted catalyst that uses exceptional travel experiences as a context to engage, motivate and/or recognize people for increased levels of personal commitment and extraordinary performance - irrespective of whatever they do or wherever they work.

Whether they be traditional Qualifiers or system-relevant Beneficiaries.

Incentive Travel is a fascinating instrument that may also be employed to tackle many scientific, economic, organizational, health, social and ecological challenges - given expert planning, an ethical approach, clear communications, professional organisation, and memorable trip delivery.

Indeed, Incentive Travel has proven over the past half-century that it can quite imaginatively and robustly adapt to changing circumstances and expanding global geographies.

The Incentive Travel sector will remain a significant vehicle for both live and hybrid events post-Covid - because it remains one of the most cost-effective, successful, and enjoyable options for inspiring and connecting people from all over the world.

Changes only happen when we ourselves drive them onwards.

So, let's get our personal and collective thinking caps on, and move forward with confidence and certainty, remembering always that we are not alone, and that *Incentive Travel for a New World* is indeed:

"A very special tool that uses an exceptional travel experience to motivate, recognize and / or reward individuals for exemplary levels of engagement, performance and achievement in support of either organisational, scientific, climate, environmental or societal goals."

APPENDIX I

Incentive Goals By Branch

The following is a summary of the central incentive goals pursued by the *Finance & Insurance, Automotive, Consumer Electronics* and *Pharmaceuticals* branches pre-Covid.

It is still important to understand these and to always bear them in mind.

Finance & Insurance

Business with finance and insurance products and services is characterised by trust and relationships. Personal contacts and customer consultation are important.

If trust is broken, customers will take their business elsewhere.

The *central incentive goal* for finance and insurance companies is the employment of appropriate rewards that allow them to remain attractive employers and maintain customer loyalty.

The latter particularly in the light of online banking and comparison portals.

Sustainable customer loyalty is the primary goal of all this effort.

Allied to this, is gaining the loyalty of and incentivising independent finance dealers and insurance brokers to both recommend and sell financial and insurance products above and beyond competitors' offerings.

Automotive

Automotive brands are well-established and world-renowned. Despite this, competition is tough – both in winning new customers and in attracting qualified employees.

This applies both to car manufacturers and to their suppliers, dealers and vehicle service partners.

The *central incentive goal* for the automotive branch is the employment of appropriate reward solutions that help generate new and additional business and which enhance its image as an employer.

Challenges for marketing and sales include a decline in the number of new car registrations, a reduction in classic marketing budgets and increased price and model competition (e.g., *e-mobility*).

In addition, highly dissected distribution and partner networks must be managed and optimised.

This is all rounded off by the fact that automotive manufacturers are not only interested in selling vehicles but also in developing and nurturing long-term relationships and sustainable bonds with both dealers and customers.

Consumer Electronics

This branch is characterised by complex distribution, point of sale and online networks.

The primary trend in consumer electronics is *"connectivity"*.

Smartphone sales are on the rise while turnover of other devices is declining.

Large global consumer brands dominate the market.

The *central incentive goal* for the consumer electronics branch is to discover appropriate reward solutions that reach customers, distributors, and employees.

Challenges for marketing and sales include high marketing and advertising spends.

Multi-tiered distribution networks make it more difficult for manufacturers to influence customers' purchasing decisions online or at Point of Sale.

On-going partner dialogue and binding of distributors via incentive measures are, therefore, even more important for sales promotion.

Point of Sale and online promotions must also be relevant and appealing to specific target groups to attract new and hopefully loyal customers.

Pharmaceuticals

The pharmaceuticals and life sciences industries are important sectors that traditionally generate a great deal of MICE business - from classic congresses to largescale Incentive Travel programmes.

The pharmaceuticals sector is currently undergoing rapid change as patents expire, prices fall, and global competition increases.

The pharmaceuticals industry requires extensive experience, interdisciplinary expertise, and an understanding of where this industry is at and where it is heading to.

With pharmaceutical events you must distinguish as to whether the qualifiers / trip participants are either doctors or pharmaceutical company employees and / or pharmaceuticals distributors.

The so-called *"Pharmacodex"* does not apply to the latter group, i.e., pharmaceutical company employees and pharmaceuticals distributors.

The following trends are characteristic for MICE events for pharmaceutical company employees and pharmaceuticals distributors:

· Shorter duration.

· Shorter distances and travel times.

· Good access and central locations required.

· More conference, more training, more coaching, fewer social programmes.

with

· Lots of workshops and breakout sessions.

· Toned-down evening functions.

· Shorter lead-in times and planning horizons.

MICE event activity in the pharmaceuticals sector is independent of the general market / economic situation but dependent upon the success and product cycle stage of individual pharmaceutical products.

Strict understanding and observance of the *"Pharma-codex"*, i.e., less expenditure, no 5-star products, simple food & beverage services, no social programmes, no accompanying persons is essential.

Destinations chosen are dependent upon the scientific or medical association organiser's decisions and choice.

QR Code: EFPIA - *European Federation of Pharmaceutical Industries and Associations*

APPENDIX II

Traditional Benefits Of Incentive Travel

As we enter the post-Covid era - where much is unknown and still in the balance - it is worth re-considering what *bis dato* have been the traditional benefits of Incentive Travel for corporations and companies.

Sales & Distribution

Problems experienced by companies often included too many leads for too few salespeople, no influence upon consumer behaviour at points of sale, pressure on turnover and profit margins from direct competitors.

Solutions included employing an external force of sales & distribution partners (*dealers*).

Differentiated incentives for these (*travel, cash, vouchers*) were often deciding factors in achieving competitive advantage and business success.

Customer Relationships

"Return on Relationship" (Ted Rubin*)* incentives were especially effective in branches where customer relationships either extended over a long period of time or where there was high frequency contact over a short period of time.

Both instances were sometimes prone to periods of inactivity - and to possibilities of dissatisfaction and a desire for change.

The challenge was to keep customers on board and clients satisfied and to keep them convinced.

If customer expectations were surpassed by an unexpected incentive, there was a good chance that they would remain loyal.

Customer Loyalty

There are two ways to grow business – win new customers and / or keep current customers.

The latter is cost efficient, and this is where Customer Relationship Management comes into play.

This, in the past meant turning new customers into happy customers and maintaining customer bonds with incentives that showed appreciation and gratitude for continued loyalty.

New Clients

Marketing and sales managers have two possibilities to generate growth - either acquire new customers or retain existing customers.

Winning new customers in strongly competitive markets is always a big challenge.

How can a company attract customers away from competitors and generate additional turnover with products, services, and brands?

Pre-Covid, it was necessary to create attractive incentives to generate and maintain interest and to strengthen purchasing patterns.

Employee Satisfaction

Motivation is derived from the Latin verb *"movere"* – to move.

Only when employees* were moved to perform was corporate success believed to be guaranteed.

*Note: Not managers - the persons frequently quoted

in representative studies as the primary reason for poor employee motivation.

Motivation arose because of appreciation and recognition. Companies who offered the right incentives were taken seriously by employees and management roles were strengthened.

Incentive packages were also decisive in attracting and binding scarce talent and at the same time spreading positive word-of-mouth messages to potential employees in times of skill shortages.

Employees, who experienced appreciation and recognition tended to work harder - or so it was believed - took fewer days off, seldom resigned and were more engaged.

"Individual Incentives" as opposed to group travel incentives also played a role – and were not only linked to individual performance but to specific occasions and personal anniversaries.

This way, companies could visibly show that they valued and appreciated their employees.

TIP: *"ENGAGE for SUCCESS"*

Have a look at the following *"Get Engaged"* video on employee engagement and motivation in the workplace. This is a good *UK Government* campaign video.

QR Code: *Engage for Success*

(*YouTube* video)

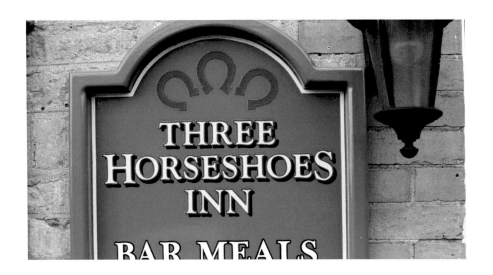

FURTHER INFORMATION

Best-Practice & Topical Research

IRU - Incentive Research Foundation

https://theirf.org/research/

SITE – Society for Incentive Travel Excellence

https://www.siteglobal.com

SITE Foundation Research

https://siteglobal.com/about-site-foundation

Incentive Travel Industry Index - Regional & Sectoral

Reports on Incentive Travel

https://siteglobal.com/incentive-travel-industry-index

SITE CITP Certification

https://siteglobal.com/citp

ibtm World Research

https://ibtmevents.com/category/blog/mice-industry/

imex Group Research

https://www.imexexhibitions.com/research

ITB Berlin Research

https://news.itb.com/industry-news/topics/business-travel-mice/

ima - incentive marketing association europe

http://www.imaeurope.com/

vdvo - Verband der Veranstaltungsorganisatoren - Studies

https://vdvo.de/kategorien/studien/

GCB - German Convention Bureau Research

https://www.gcb.de/de/trends-inspiration/meeting-eventbarometer.html

Five Incentive Travel Trends to Watch

https://meetingstoday.com/articles/142830/5-incentive-travel-trends-watch

Incentive Roundtable Reveals Travel Trends and Challenges

https://www.northstarmeetingsgroup.com/Incentive/Strategy/Incentive-Travel-Trends-Roundtable-2021

ICCA World Market Research

https://www.iccaworld.org/knowledge/10/Industry-research

China MICE Market Study

https://www.readkong.com/page/china-mice-market-study-a-report-on-the-characteristics-and-5979728

ETOA - European Tourism Association Research

https://www.etoa.org/research/

UNWTO Tourism Statistics Data

https://www.unwto.org/tourism-statistics-data

MICE knowledge

https://www.miceknowledge.com/lets-start-the-journey/

Padraicino - A Blog about Destinations and Matters related to the Meetings Industry

https://padraicino.com/

Ted Rubin - Return on Relationship

https://tedrubin.com/return-relationship-ror-ronr/

Select Trade Press

CIM - Conference & Incentive Management

https://www.cimunity.com/

TW - Tagungswirtschaft

https://www.tw-media.com/

M&IT - Meetings & Incentive Travel

https://mitmagazine.co.uk/

Incentive - What Motivates

https://www.northstarmeetingsgroup.com/Incentive

Corporate & Incentive Travel

https://www.themeetingmagazines.com/corporate-
incentive-travel/

Meetings International

https://www.meetingsinternational.com/

The China Guide - MICE Travel

https://www.thechinaguide.com/de/mice

China Travel News

https://www.chinatravelnews.com/mice/

MICE China

http://www.micechina.com

MICE Showcase (*India*)

https://www.miceshowcase.com/

QR Code: *Report on MICE Market in India (.pdf)*

DR. PATRICK PATRIDGE

Tourism, Marketing & PR Consultant
SITE Member since 1990
Jane E. Schuldt Master Motivator Award 2017
SITE Kevin Forde Spirit Award 2010
Past-President SITE Germany
Speaker & Author, Historian & Geographer
Born in Dublin and living in Frankfurt am Main

ABOUT THE FRONTISPIECE

I arrived to live and work in Frankfurt am Main on the 9th of November 1988, exactly a year to the day before the Fall of the Berlin Wall.

Or *Mauerfall*, as it is known in Germany.

Construction of the Berlin Wall began on 13th August 1961. 60 years later, this book on INCENTIVE TRAVEL was written.

From darkness into light.

To mark the occasion, I asked my daughter Paula to create an original frontispiece with reference to a *Berlin Wall Grafitto* I photographed in late-March 1985 in Berlin-Kreuzberg, during the course of a University College Dublin Geography Department student excursion, led by the remarkable and inspirational, Prof. Dr. Anngret Simms.

Paula has included a side view of the face of one of the colourful, original Berlin Wall graffiti characters in her new picture.

Bringing him back to life, so to say, because the original is lost to posterity.

See if you can spot him - and his buddy - in the original photograph from March 1985.

BOOKS BY THIS AUTHOR

GERMAN CUISINE
WINES & BEERS

A Brief Introduction

There is no better way for you to explore Germany and its regions than by eating German food and drinking German beers and wines. Something special is available for every occasion and palate – from authentic locally sourced fresh food to high-end Michelin-star cuisine.

Traditional German cooking varies in menus and style from one city and region to the next and is really great value for money. Its diversity is a result of Germany's history and colourful landscapes, each region having its own traditional food restaurants, home-grown recipes, beer, and wine festivals.

A perfect Room Gift for guests and for Incentive Travel partici-pants visiting Germany.

Available from *amazon* in Paperback and KindleUnlimited edi-tions.

BERLIN WALL

Recollections 1983 - 2020

"Patrick's reflections on Berlin are superb and rich in detail - it is the layering of time and places and thereby the dissolving of the rigidity of temporal and geographical borders that make his recollections particularly enjoyable. You can really see the geographer at work, tracing the memoryscapes of Berlin and Dublin over one another until they overlap."

Margaret Haverly

Ph.D. Scholar at *Konrad Adenauer Stiftung, University of Tübingen*

BERLIN WALL

I was thinking about what a wonderful city Berlin was to experience, whether as part of a study group tour, or simply exploring by myself. Over the years. There was always something, somewhere or somebody different to discover and to see. No matter how many times you visited - whether for family, work, leisure, or friends. Lots of history and plenty of architectural and cultural variety. Never a dull moment.

My mind was suddenly crowded with vivid recollections, private musings, colourful *vignettes*, and a powerful sense of place. Mostly - but certainly by no means exclusively - focusing upon visits to the Berlin Wall and associations therewith from my first ever visit in 1983 to its almost invisibility today; from the Iron Curtain, trips to West and East Berlin, the Fall of The Wall and German Re-Unification.

And all from an Irish perspective.

A perfect Room Gift for guests and for Incentive Travel participants visiting Berlin.

Available from *amazon* in Paperback and KindleUnlimited editions.

FOOTSTEPS

Poetry & Prose 1987 - 2021

"You captured my generation and experiences so well and I found so many images and memories resonated with me."

Patrick Delaney

soolnua

"The vividly rendered details of memoryscapes and everyday life are extremely evocative ... a powerful document of the life of an Irish person in Germany. FOOTSTEPS speaks to many people for so many idiosyncratic reasons."

Margaret Haverty

Ph.D. Scholar at *Konrad Adenauer Stiftung, University of Tübingen*

"I finished reading FOOTSTEPS this evening and really enjoyed

it. The poetry and prose is a nice combination. I appreciate the Irish references being from Dublin - and the German ones, too. My brother lived in Berlin in the mid-90s - and I have also visited a number of other German cities. On the Irish side, I particularly enjoyed UCD days. I went to DCU but could also relate to the academic context - and to the menace of the Dublin-Monaghan bombings (I keep thinking of the song 'Raised by Wolves' by U2). Of course, the tribute to Grove DJ, Cecil Nolan, was great, too."

Brian Tucker

The Grove Radio Show

FOOTSTEPS - Poetry & Prose 1987 - 2021

This is a compendium about the delights of spoken language and the magic of living words. A playful variety of poetry styles and contemporary prose.

Written in Dublin-English in Germany - with a tiny spattering of Gaelic and German in between! A potpourri of fantasy, fact and veritable fiction spanning six decades from Ireland to Germany.

For a quiet rainy-day muse or to be read out aloud in the warm summer sun! Anecdotes and episodes recalling among many other themes:

Teenage Dublin Walkabouts, love and affection, a haunted Rhine-land castle, Celtic Mythology, Guardian Angels, Bono's wedding reception, UCD Days, The Grove Social Club, Victorian Dublin, Car Bombs in Dublin, Count Dracula, The Good Friday Agreement, Santa's New Grotto, Gulf WarSpeak, Salsa dancing in Frankfurt, the Eurovision Song Contest, an Errant Medieval Knight and the vagaries of Life, the Universe and Everything.

Distilling thoughts, experiences and miscellaneous impressions gleaned over the years - both in Germany and in Ireland.

Characterised by light-hearted observations, philosophical meanderings, tongue-in-cheek banter, and surreal metaphysical debate. Footsteps gathering pace, so to say, accompanied by quiet recollection, personal reminiscence, and subtle reflection.

Written both in Dublin, the place of my youth, and in Frankfurt am Main, my adoptive new home.

REVIEW

PROSE: Like 'Ulysses', its puns and punditry, and its stream-of-consciousness perambulations compete and contrast abruptly with bold outbursts of straight prose and memoir of life before, during and after early schooling, university education and subsequent experience.

Covering decades of observation, with reference to history, culture, religion, and mythology, including, at times, very cryptic allusion. It might be read and/or spoken aloud like a self-contained, one-person show.

Although its geography and tangents leap from Europe to Asia and even as far as the heavenly realm of angels and archangels, this is at heart an energetic discourse in latter day Dublinosity.

POETRY: Well captured - the imagery of place and time and the complex weave of history, folklore, personal memoir and myth; obviously of Dublin and Germany and even ancient Gaul, but also of the deeper Irish layers of origin, from geology and topography through place names and tradition, up to the fleeting present.

There is the same Joycean allusion as in the prose, but not necessarily as Dublin-centric. It forces the reader to think of the value of time and place in the lives of everyone, passing through.

Patrick Long M.A.

Historian, Museum Curator & Contributor to the *Dictionary of Irish Biography*

Available from amazon in Hardcover, Paperback and KindleUnlimited editions.

A perfect Room Gift for guests and for Incentive Travel participants visiting Ireland and Germany.

Made in United States
Orlando, FL
30 May 2023